Helicopters, Jets, and Bush Planes

My Flying Life, From Vietnam to Alaska

Chuck Moore

8370 Eleusis Drive, Anchorage, Alaska 99502-4630
books@publicationconsultants.com—www.publicationconsultants.com

ISBN Number: 978-1-59433-964-6
eBook ISBN Number: 978-1-59433-965-3

Library of Congress Number: 2025913771

Copyright © 2025 Chuck Moore
—First Edition—

All rights reserved, including the right of reproduction in any form, or by any mechanical or electronic means including photocopying or recording, or by any information storage or retrieval system, in whole or in part in any form, and in any case not without the written permission of the author.

Manufactured in the United States of America

TABLE OF CONTENTS

Introduction 5

PART ONE: UNITED STATES ARMY 1966–1973

1. Army Life and Boot Camp 16
2. US Army Rotary Wing Aviator Course 21
3. Vietnam 37
4. After Vietnam 63
5. College 67

PART TWO: UNITED STATES NAVY 1974–1992

6. Navy Life 74
7. Naval Aviation Schools Command Flight School 79
8. Arriving in California and Aircraft Carrier Operations 87
9. Airline Pilot 113
10. Back in the US Navy 124

PART THREE: ALASKA 1993–2025

11. Alaska Bush Pilot 136
12. US Government Pilot 161
13. Alaska Aerobatics 175
14. Private Pilot 183

INTRODUCTION

1947–1965
Early Childhood to Age Eighteen

This is the story of my life, as I remember it. I always thought it was pretty typical, until, in my seventies, people started telling me that it wasn't. And that I needed to write it down. So here is what I remember.

I was born in 1947 in Parkersburg, West Virginia, the oldest son of the oldest son of Pete and Winnie Moore. My grandpa was a great man, a pipe smoker, and a farmer who was a churchgoer. I never knew him to drink or curse, and he loved his children and grandchildren. He and Winnie had six children, my dad being the first. Raised in a small town, Dad was a star athlete and desired by all the girls in the little high school in Cairo, West Virginia. He was also a hero to his younger siblings—three brothers and two sisters. The United States entered World War Two in 1941, so like many young men, after graduating from high school in 1942, he joined the US Army, along with his high school buddy, and teammate, Don Kirkpatrick. Their girlfriends were sisters. All of them, except my mother, were in the same class. She was a freshman when they were seniors. Dad's name was Charles, but he went by his middle name, Harold. He spent twenty-four months with the US Army Air Corps as a radio operator/gunner in the 8th Air Force, stationed at Rackheath Airfield in England during WWII. After his thirty-five missions over Germany or occupied territories in a B-24 Liberator heavy bomber, without being shot down or captured, he returned to America, and in a double ceremony, married his high school sweetheart, my mother, Annabelle, and Don married her sister, Ermalee.

After returning home to West Virginia, Dad got into a union and learned welding, pipe fitting, and lead burning. At that time, Union Carbide, a large chemical company, now part of the Dow Chemical Company, was building new plants in the northeast. They used a lot of lead-lined pipes. It took about three months for my dad's work to be finished, and then we moved to the next city that was getting a new plant. I remember going to two different schools most years, so I have no childhood friends, except for my cousins.

The house that we lived in when I was born was a small wood-frame house with no plumbing, except for a pitcher pump on the counter, which was attached to a well under the kitchen. Over the next several years, we lived in various rented houses located near the small towns in the hills of western West Virginia. Around 1955, when I was eight, my father decided that we should get a mobile home, which was commonly called a trailer, since we were moving so often for his work. I remember my parents and us four children living in a 32-foot-long, eight-foot-wide trailer for a few years. 256 square feet! Today that would be called an RV travel trailer. Later we got a 52-foot-long, ten-foot-wide trailer, which was much better. I remember the trailer park life well, but not fondly.

With one car, which my dad took to work every day, we were either in school or at the trailer park. I remember a couple of them catching fire from the wall-mounted heaters. The preservative on the wood paneling was formaldehyde, which you could smell, and it was toxic and flammable. So the trailers burned hot and fast, leaving nothing salvageable. I'm certain that people died in trailer fires in those days. We lived in several states, including Ohio, Delaware, and Tennessee.

One memorable Saturday, we were all at home in our trailer, except for Dad, when someone banged on the door. My mother opened it, and a woman crawled in and lay moaning on the living room floor. She was

INTRODUCTION

covered in blood and had obviously been beaten. It was at the hands of her husband, Whitey Ford, my dad's best friend. Mom cleaned her up, and after a while, she went back to her trailer minus a few teeth. The linoleum floor made the cleanup easier.

Mom's mother, our grandmother, Myrtle Rose Fisher, lived with us in West Virginia in the early 1950s, for a few years before I was old enough to go to school. I was four or five years old. Our dog, Perky, was a beautiful Collie. At that time, we had a large two-story house on Route 50, outside of Parkersburg, with enough acreage to have a large lawn to play in, a big garden, an apple orchard, and a small barn for two milk cows and a couple of dozen chickens. We also raised a couple of pigs every year to butcher. We had beehives that we got lots of honey from. Mom would sell some, along with butter that she churned and eggs. I remember the door-to-door salesmen selling encyclopedias and Fuller brushes. One salesman was demonstrating his unbreakable dishes. When he tried to bounce a cup off the floor, the handle broke off. Mom didn't buy any dishes. Later, when I was in the Army, I noticed that the dishes were all brown but made of the exact same material. A Google search revealed them as polycarbonate mess hall dishes. Today's military doesn't have mess halls but dining facilities. Why do we have to constantly change the names of everything?

Anyway, someone heard that bee venom would relieve arthritis pain. In addition to other health problems, Grandma had crippling arthritis in her hands that was very painful. So Dad went to the beehives and collected a mason jar full of bees. We all watched as he picked each one up with tweezers and held them on Grandma's knuckles to sting her. I also remember that the relief only lasted until the pain from the stings subsided! Every Easter, us kids would get baby chicks or ducks that had been dyed in bright reds, greens, and purples. They were beautiful! When they grew up Mom butchered them but they didn't run around the yard after their heads were chopped off, like the chickens did!

In 1957, when I was ten, and there were five of us children now, my dad decided to move out west. He wanted to be closer to his high school and Army Air Corps buddy, my Uncle Don Kirkpatrick. Mom was happy to live near her mother and sister, too. I don't know what encouraged my Uncle Don to move out west, but he was a school administrator in Farmington, New Mexico. My Grandma Fisher had moved with them and now lived with the Kirkpatricks. Aunt Ermalee had six children, so that made nine in their family. Grandma Fisher was a wonderful person who was cherished by all of us, and she loved her family. She was widowed before any of us grandchildren were born, so we never knew our mother's father. Unfortunately, Grandma was stricken with polio at an early age, so she was confined to a wheelchair. She still managed to raise her three daughters by having boarders and giving piano lessons, with her oldest, Ermalee, performing most of the motherly duties.

To make our move to New Mexico, Dad bought a 1947 Chevrolet pickup, with a couple of feet chopped off the back to make it shorter and easier for towing trailers. It had a trailer brake control attached to the steering column that you pushed with your knee while your foot pushed the regular brake pedal. The truck had a six-cylinder engine, so it took a while to tow that fifty-two-foot trailer across the Rockies! I can't imagine doing that today. In those days, vehicles would overheat climbing the mountains in the summer, so you had to stop and let them cool off occasionally and add water to the radiator. The water barrels with signs saying "radiator water," in remote locations on the mountain highways in hot country, are still there.

For some reason, I was given a lot of responsibility as a young boy still in grade school. For instance, helping set up the gifts after my brothers and sisters had gone to sleep on Christmas Eve. Mom or Dad would quietly enter my bedroom, which I shared with my brother, and wake me up. The Christmas presents were always kept in the trunk of our car, parked outside in front of our trailer. I would help carry them in and set them up under the tree. Then I'd get cookies and milk for Santa before going back to bed.

When I was about ten years old, I got a paper route. After school every day, I would pick up my bundle of papers from the curb, then

INTRODUCTION

take them to my room to roll each one and put green rubber bands on them. If it was raining, I had to put them in a waxed paper envelope after rolling them. Then I would put all of them into the white cotton pouches that were connected. There was an opening in the middle to put your head through. There would be a pouch in front and one in the back like a backpack. After putting it on, I would ride my bicycle to the first house at the highest point on my route and start throwing the papers as close to the front doors as I could get as I coasted down the street.

Occasionally, one would land on the roof, and I would have to throw another one. The newspaper company always included a few extras for this reason. I would throw on one side and then the other until I got to the last one. Collection night was Thursday night, and I had a big metal ring with a stiff paper card for each customer. I also had a metal punch to make a hole in the card to show that the weekly fee was paid. Occasionally, I was told by a customer that they didn't have the thirty-five cents. So I had to pay for their papers.

A couple of years later, when I got my motorbike, I would use it to throw papers while riding very slowly. That made the job a lot more fun! Before a paperboy went on vacation with his family, he would take a friend who also had a newspaper route and show him your route. This was because every house did not get a paper—only those that paid for a subscription. So he would throw his route and yours until you got back. You would do the same for him when he went on vacation with his family.

In 1959, when I was twelve, I started driving a tractor for a man my dad worked with, plowing fields on his farm in Colorado on weekends. He and his wife would pick me up at my house after school on Fridays and drive a few hours to his farm. It was a small farm, where he planted wheat and beans. There was an old one-bedroom log cabin with a wood-burning stove that was used for heating and cooking. His wife would cook the meals while he and I were out in the fields all day, plowing with his two tractors. They were Farmall H models. She even made pies from the cherry trees in the middle of the field. Then we drove back home on Sunday evening. I was paid two dollars per hour, cash. I saved my money.

Helicopters, Jets, and Bush Planes

In New Mexico, you could get a license to operate a motorcycle or scooter with a small engine at the age of thirteen. I saw an advertisement in the newspaper for a used motorbike. It was a small Harley-Davidson. I talked my dad into going to look at it with me one evening. The owner started it up, and I rode it down the street and back. I paid him seventy-five dollars for it. We took it home, but as much as I tried, I couldn't get it started again. I don't remember what eventually happened to it, but one Saturday, out of the blue, Dad asked me if I wanted to go look at motorcycles. We went to a motorcycle dealership and found the one I wanted. I still remember riding it home. It was a brand-new 1961, 175 cc Ducati, red and gold. Beautiful! Then I made payments for that. I remember riding it to the hospital for Grandma to see. I looked up from the parking lot to see her looking out of her window several floors up. Waving and seeing her waving back is my last memory of her. She died a few weeks later. I was thirteen, so she was probably still in her fifties.

School was easy, and I only got straight As until I took geometry in my sophomore year in high school in 1963. I remember back in Tennessee, while still in grade school, the teacher had a spelling bee once a week. Everyone would stand by their desk until you missed a word; then you would sit down. I was always the last one standing. The winner received a token for a free ice cream bar at lunch. Now I feel guilty for not purposely misspelling a word occasionally. They didn't have a chance with my phonics skills!

When I was fourteen, I got a job at a Dr Pepper bottling plant. There were only two of us. My boss, the manager and bottler, and me, the bottle washer. The challenge was keeping up with the conveyor that carried the bottles to the washing machine. It never stopped moving, and it was pretty fast. I always worked after school and on weekends. I was never involved in any school activities or attended any sporting events. We never had extra money for school yearbooks, but I recently bought a used one online for my high school graduation year. Next to the pictures of my classmates was a list of their many extracurricular activities, like sports teams, bands, and various clubs. The space next to my picture is blank.

INTRODUCTION

Mom was a church member, and Dad would drop us all off at the church and then pick us up after, as we only had one vehicle that we could all fit into, our red and white 1958 Ford. Cars were usually painted in two colors then. They called it two-tone. Actually, we still had the old pickup, and when Dad would drive it to work, he would take the rotor out of the distributor on the car, so Mom couldn't go anywhere. A guy who was a few years older than me, Charlie Smith, befriended me, and he would drive the two of us to church in his 1954 Ford. Then we would have dinner at his house with his parents and brother, JD. He raised rabbits and had pigeons. We often killed and cleaned a rabbit, which his mother would barbecue for Sunday dinner. I remember after I turned fifteen, I got my own car, and JD, who later became a chiropractor, rebuilt the engine in my old Ford. He pulled the engine out with a rope and pulley system and hung it in a tree in his backyard. I later learned that Charlie Smith would always mentor a young boy, setting an example of how to be a good man. I lost contact with him but will never forget him.

One spring day, he dropped me off at my house after church. The rest of the family was already there. As usual, I headed to my bedroom, which I shared with my brother, while removing my tie. My brothers and sisters were in the living room. It was immediately apparent that Mom and Dad were fighting again. I was in the narrow hallway of our small house, a few feet from my bedroom door, when Mom ran past me with Dad not far behind. When Dad got beside me, I saw that Mom had grabbed my brother's .22 rifle from its rack above his bed. She immediately turned toward us and fired. She didn't aim, but the bullet entered Dad's upper face and stopped in his brain. I have a vivid memory of the blood shooting out and hitting the white wooden door frame. Dad lay there making strange sounds as I just looked at him and called to him, too scared to touch him. The other kids stayed in the living room. Mom went to the kitchen phone and called for help. An ambulance eventually came and took him to the hospital. We stayed with my Uncle Don and Aunt Ermalee for several days. Dad died that night, he was thirty-eight. It was April 28, 1963. I was fifteen, in my sophomore year of high school. The school board excused me and my siblings from going back to school for the year.

Helicopters, Jets, and Bush Planes

I, being the only witness, testified at a court hearing about what happened. Mom was not charged with anything. A couple of months later, after settling her affairs in New Mexico, she took the rest of the family to Idaho so she could attend college there. She had always wanted to be a nurse, so she found a school and enrolled at the age of thirty-six. Over the next few years, she got a nursing degree, then went to California to get a master's degree. She became a professor of nursing at the University of Alaska in Anchorage. She applied for a teaching position there because Don and Ermalee and their family had moved to Alaska during the years that my mother was in school. She became the first tenured professor in the University of Alaska's School of Nursing and eventually retired.

I had taken Driver's Ed in high school, allowing me to get my regular driver's license at fifteen. I remember the driver's education instructor having me take a few of the other students to teach them how to parallel park by myself. None of us had a license, so we were supposed to stay in the school parking lot. Of course, under my instructions, we headed to the Dairy Queen downtown! I don't think the teacher ever knew about it.

When Dad died, Mom started driving his car, and I got hers. Then I got a job in a grocery store across town. I started as a bagger at age sixteen. A few months later, I was promoted to cashier. That same year, I was also given my own department, responsible for all the frozen foods, and I did all of the ordering and stocking. I admit that, when in my walk-in freezer in the back of the store, I would occasionally chow down on a frozen pie or something! Boy, it was cold in there. One morning, my brother and I decided not to go to school. About an hour after my mom left for work, a police officer came to our house and took me and my brother to jail. We were in there for three days before she bailed us out. We were real criminals, skipping school! I was extremely embarrassed to explain it to my boss, the owner of the grocery store.

Before Mom sold our house and moved to Idaho, I got an apartment with one of the older guys at the store, Jimmy, who was several years older than me. In those days, the high schools had shop classes. Wood shop and metal shop. In wood shop, with Charlie Smith's help,

INTRODUCTION

I built a gun cabinet of curly maple wood, lined with red velveteen, for my dad. It was beautiful. Needing money, I sold it to Jimmy for fifty dollars. I wish I still had it.

Being on my own at sixteen, I started missing more and more days at school and finally dropped out in 1964, my junior year of high school, to work full-time. Several months later, in the summer of 1965, I could see that I had no future without finishing high school, so I quit my job and drove to Boise, Idaho, where my mother was going to college. I needed fewer credits to graduate there.

During that summer, I got a job as a driver's helper on a garbage truck in the city of Boise. It paid eighty dollars a week. We started at five o'clock in the morning and were finished by noon. I would cover my side of the street and the driver his. There were two trash cans on the side of each house that had to be carried on your shoulder to the truck, one at a time. And the driver was fast, a very hard worker. I was a skinny teenager, and at the end of the day, I was worn out. I spent the winter living with my family in a small Boise Junior College campus apartment while finishing high school. As soon as I got the credits, I left. It was the end of the first semester, just before Christmas, 1965, so there was no graduation ceremony; I just quit going.

After an argument with my mother one day, I said that if I had twenty dollars I would leave. She handed me a twenty-dollar bill, and I left. Gas was about twenty-five cents a gallon, so I headed back to New Mexico. Around midnight, I was too tired to keep going, so I pulled over by a city park in Salt Lake City, Utah. It was cold, so I left my engine running for the heater. About two or three o'clock in the morning, I was awakened by a tapping noise on my driver's side window. I rolled it down, and a police officer asked me my name. After I told him, he said, "Okay, your mom was worried about you." Amazing!

After getting to Farmington the next day, I went to see the apartment manager who had rented to me and Jimmy. She was an older single lady, and I will never forget her. Sitting on her porch, I explained my situation. I had nowhere to go and no money. I told her that I had a week's pay coming from the garbage company, and she let me have an apartment. The next day, I went back to the grocery store and got my old job back. I loved my mother, but we were like oil and water. I regret not being able to get along with her. Once, when I was leaving unexpectedly, she told me that I was the only one of her children that she would die for.

Several months later, I sold my car and rode a Greyhound bus to Ohio to live with my Uncle Charlie and his wife, my dad's younger sister, Pattie. I missed my dad's family and my Grandpa Moore. I soon got a job at a gas station and was enjoying spending time with my dad's family again. I got another car, a rusty 1956 Chevrolet with a six-cylinder engine and three on the tree. It was two-tone green and ran fine, but it had a lot of rust holes in it. I paid a hundred dollars for it. We sold tires at the gas station, so I put new tires on it. They cost me more than the car! I drove it to my grandparents' house in a little town in the hills of West Virginia, Harrisville, every weekend.

Back in high school in New Mexico, I had learned how to play the guitar from a friend, another Charles Smith. Eventually, I joined a band and started playing at different places on weekends. Sock hops were popular. They were held in the school gymnasium, where no shoes were allowed, except for gym shoes. Since we didn't carry those around, kids just danced in their socks. We also played at the roller rink and the Knights of Columbus Hall.

While living in Ohio with my aunt and uncle and working at the gas station, I met a few students at Marietta College who had a band. One day, they asked if I could play with them at a concert at the college. They didn't have a rhythm guitar player. I said sure. The artist was Engelbert Humperdinck, a popular singer at the time. We were the warm-up band. Hundreds of college students were there, and it was really fun performing. But my life was about to take a different path.

PART ONE

United States Army
1966–1973
Ages Nineteen to Twenty-Six

CHAPTER ONE
Army Life and Boot Camp

In the summer of 1966, while enjoying my time in West Virginia, I got my draft notice. I guess the government noticed that I was over eighteen and was not enrolled in school. I had just turned nineteen. So I drove my hundred-dollar car over 2,000 miles, back to Idaho. As a teenager, I had driven my car across the country before, so that was not a problem. There I enrolled in the junior college in Boise and applied for a student deferral. The pastor of the First Baptist Church that I attended also wrote a letter, saying that my mother had already given the Army one son, my younger brother, Paul. I wasn't opposed to joining or going to Vietnam; I just wanted a little more time to think about it. One night, I let my little sister borrow my car. She called a couple of hours later wanting a ride home. So, I borrowed my mother's car and picked her up. She had let her boyfriend drive it, and he rolled it over, destroying it. Nothing from insurance; I didn't even get my practically new tires back! Turns out I wouldn't need a car for a while anyway.

At Christmas time, my younger brother, who had dropped out of high school and joined the Army a year before, at seventeen, came home on leave. He told me that, as a high school graduate, I could be an Army helicopter pilot and to go and see the recruiter who enlisted him. After he went back from his Army leave, I went to see Staff Sergeant Lane in downtown Boise. Sergeant Lane gave me a book to study before taking the exam for flight training. I had never been on an aircraft before, not even a commercial airline flight. In those days, we traveled by bus, Greyhound, or Trailways. I studied the book and passed the exam. Then he sent me to Salt Lake City, Utah, where I was interviewed by a panel of Army officers and pilots. I was accepted. At the end of flight school, if you were successful and graduated, you would be promoted from E-5, a student pilot's pay grade, to WO-1, a warrant officer. It was a significant change in pay and rank. Unlike a commissioned officer like a lieutenant, your primary job was flying helicopters. For commissioned officers who were pilots, flying was a secondary duty, managing men being the first.

So, in December 1966, I got on a bus and was off to Fort Polk, Louisiana, for basic training, unofficially known as boot camp. I was nineteen. Most infantrymen were sent to Ft. Polk, and I read that a million soldiers were trained there during the Vietnam War. It was December, so most of the staff was on Christmas leave when the new recruits arrived. For several days, we had little supervision. While hanging out in the barracks with all the other recruits, I met Bob Nance and Jim Cozine. We are still friends today. Military men form lifelong bonds and consider each other as brothers. Jim became a two-star general. He lives in Boise, Idaho, where he grew up, still married to his high school sweetheart. They were married before Jim went to Vietnam. My last name was Moore, and we were always lined up alphabetically, so Nance and I ended up doing everything together. We had the same primary flight school instructor and spent a lot of our four years in the Army together. We are best friends to this day and see each other every year, almost sixty years later.

Winter in Louisiana was wet and cold. Spinal meningitis was going around, so we had to be an arms length apart at all times. We were also required to sit in every other seat in the auditorium. There were about two hundred men in each company, which was made up of four platoons of forty men, plus officers and sergeants. Each platoon was divided into four squads of ten men. So we were with the same men in our platoon at all times, with no freedom to go anywhere individually, until the completion of eight weeks of basic training. We had to have a fire guard stay on duty at night because we were living in old wooden

WWII barracks, two-story buildings housing forty men. The first floor had a large shower room and rows of washbasins and toilets. With no partitions, there was zero privacy. All military units, operating on a 24/7/365 schedule, had every soldier take a turn at being a sentry, duty officer, fire guard, or any of the many positions required to be manned at all times. America's military never sleeps. The normal shift was eight hours, and you would usually get the next day off. The fire guard shifts were four hours long, so we didn't get the next day off. We would wear a list of procedures to follow on a clipboard on a string around our neck. You would stand watch in your barracks, and your duty was to sound the alarm in case of fire. There is usually a duty office just inside the entrance to every major military building with an enlisted man sitting at a desk. His supervisor is a duty officer who is a commissioned or warrant officer, available during normal working hours, but otherwise, he stands his duty in his quarters, during non-working hours.

Military personnel were required to be housed on the base if there was housing available. Military housing was definitely cheaper than renting in town, so most of the junior personnel, meaning low rank and low pay, chose to live on base. The housing was very nice, with houses for families in a subdivision and barracks with individual rooms for single personnel in another area. The officers usually preferred to live off base, especially if they were single, because there were so many rules. So when they checked in to their new base, they would complete the paperwork requesting off-base housing and would wait until their name moved up on the list, when they were notified that they could move off base. But it was always a personal preference. If the officer was housed on base, he could stand his duty in his quarters. If he lived off base, he would have to stand his watch in a room at the BOQ. All bases had a BOQ, bachelor officer's quarters, and a BEQ, bachelor enlisted quarters. Later, when flying across the country on a flight requiring an RON, meaning remain overnight, my flight crew would usually stay in the BOQ or BEQ. We would get our meals in the officer or enlisted dining facilities. We never had to leave the base, which would require a rental car and extra time that we didn't have anyway. If the base quarters were full, then we'd stay at a local hotel.

CHAPTER ONE: Army Life and Boot Camp

You might have noticed that the military is organized to keep officers and enlisted personnel separate. It was shown very early in history, that allowing officers and enlisted men to get too close to each other results in discipline breaking down, and the mission suffers. So operating more like an employer and employee, rather than a brother or roommate situation, results in a far superior outcome. There are severe penalties for fraternizing, meaning getting into a personal relationship between an officer and an enlisted person. An officer was addressed by his rank and last name by enlisted personnel, and vice versa.

Back at boot camp, there were no interior walls in the barracks, just rows of metal army bunk beds with wooden foot lockers on the ends. Like the trucks and Jeeps, duffel bags and tents, they were all a flat, dark green, called olive drab, in color. These, as well as the steel wall lockers, contained all of our worldly possessions that had been issued to us by the United States Army. We learned that a person needs very little to live. The reply when a married soldier was denied special treatment was, if the Army wanted you to have a wife, they would have issued you one! The buildings were well maintained but had a drab exterior, no furnishings other than beds and lockers, and highly polished red linoleum flooring from the nineteen forties.

We were awakened at sunrise each morning by the sound of yelling and a metal trash can being beaten on with a baseball bat. Welcome to the US Army! Organized chaos. Each day consisted of the same routine. After everyone rushed to shower and shave, we hurriedly dressed in our fatigues and joined in a precise formation outside. After being led through various physical exercises by a drill instructor, we were marched to the chow hall for a quick breakfast. Nance, being a California boy and never having seen grits before, put sugar and milk on them, instead of butter, salt, and pepper. He thought it was Cream of Wheat. The day would then be filled with various activities, like marching, throwing live grenades, and shooting M14 rifles, even though the standard weapon in Vietnam was the M16.

One of the first things that impressed me about the Army was that we could have all the milk we wanted! White or chocolate. That was not the case when I was growing up. And kids love milk. I guess I was still a kid.

Helicopters, Jets, and Bush Planes

We were occasionally assigned KP, or kitchen police duty. Washing dishes, filling the large potato peeling machine, or refilling the milk dispensers. We didn't hand peel the potatoes, but we did use a knife to cut them into quarters. They were always boiled. I liked being the "outside man," keeping the area hosed down and clean and all of the kitchen waste organized for disposal.

One day, we were all lined up after removing our shirts to receive multiple vaccinations. These were administered by medical personnel using jet injectors, or jet guns, that used compressed air to blast the vaccine into a person's arm. They were connected to a reservoir with hundreds of doses and were very efficient because it took only a second to administer a vaccine. With a medic on either side, we got a few in both arms. Getting ready for Vietnam.

Another day, we were marched to an area where several medium-sized army tents had been set up. They had been prepared with CS gas, also called tear gas. After donning gas masks, we entered in small groups and stayed inside for a few minutes. The gas made our skin burn, but the masks allowed us to see and breathe. Standing in a circle inside the tent, we were told to remove our masks. After a minute or so, we exited through the small opening after yelling out our name, rank, and serial number to the drill instructor. Everyone was gagging and coughing. It made you appreciate your gas mask. I remember holding my breath until I was outside. Never coughed once!

Another exercise that recruits still do today includes crawling under a maze of barbed wire in the dark while live machine gun bullets are fired over your head and live grenades are exploded in dug-out areas around you. More fun and games.

Finally, after eight weeks, it was over, and we had a ceremony and picnic. Most guys were going to be eleven bravos, infantrymen, and were going to get more of the same in Tiger Land, on the same base. That's where they got their AIT, advanced infantry training. After completing their training, they would be going directly to Vietnam. A fortunate few of us were going to flight school for the next year or so.

CHAPTER TWO
US Army Rotary Wing Aviator Course

Now my goal of becoming a pilot was about to begin. After a few weeks of more military training, I would start flight training and be flying practically every day for many years to come. I reported to Fort Wolters, located near the town of Mineral Wells, Texas. It was previously known as Camp Wolters, when the most decorated soldier in US history, Audie Murphy, went there for training twenty-three years earlier. We were both nineteen years old when we were assigned there. By the time I was there, he was making Western movies, and I was just starting my military career. Now, as I approach eighty years old, I still fly and I still watch his movies.

Drill instructors, or DIs, were an elite group of handpicked soldiers. They were highly motivated, perfectly dressed and groomed, aloof but totally professional in their duties. They were sergeants so were often referred to as drill sergeants. They were responsible for training the recruits in physical fitness, military drills and formations, marching, etc. We even had them in flight school, like we did in boot camp. While we were in classes or flying all day, they would go to our rooms and arrange things for us to do when we got back. To keep us from getting bored.

Like gathering up forty pairs of spit-shined boots and making a pile of them outside in front of our building. Of course, we had our names in them, like everything else we were issued, so we could find ours, one at a time. Everyone was issued two pairs of black Army boots. That was so you could wear a fresh pair every day. They had to be spit-shined every day, too. To make sure that we didn't wear the same pair every day and use one perfectly shined pair for our inspection boots lined up under our bunks, we had to cut a notch in the heels. One pair with one notch and the other with two, so they could check for the proper pair every day during our daily formation and inspection. We didn't actually use spit but a little water in the lid of our can of Kiwi polish, and cotton balls or an old cotton T-shirt. I remember that Nance used the white T-shirts that he wore every day, just the part below the belt line! So they had black spots all around. He was one of a kind!

One day, they blocked the hallways to our rooms by carefully stacking our mattresses from the floor to the ceiling. Our three-man rooms in our flight school barracks were also inspected every day while we were in class or at the heliport. If a dead bug was found after disassembling a desk lamp, demerits were given to all the occupants of the room, and the entire platoon would have to spend their Saturday morning marching to the "cemetery," to perform a dead bug funeral. Free time in the evenings was spent studying, shining boots, and polishing brass. The uniform for that was a white T-shirt, fatigue trousers with a belt, and flip-flops. Everyone had to always be exactly the same, a well-disciplined unit. No individuality.

Primary flight school did not allow students to leave the base or drive their cars. There were several telephone booths in front of the barracks, so if you had time to stand in line for thirty minutes or more to make a five-minute limit phone call, you could call home. I don't remember ever having any time or ever calling home. In Vietnam, there weren't any telephones, so I never called home from there either. Today's warriors have cell phones in their pockets! And FaceTime!

Anytime we were outside the barracks during free time, we were subjected to harassment from upper classmen. They would stand us at attention and ask pertinent questions, like which way is north. Eventually, we would give a wrong answer and would be ordered to do pushups. Another reason I didn't go to the phone booths.

CHAPTER TWO: US ARMY ROTARY WING AVIATOR COURSE

A major part of our military training was to instill the sense that we were all together in this and would be required to act as a team at all times. We were allowed to discover this ourselves. So when one overweight or just tired soldier could not climb over a twelve-foot wall, and we all went to his aid and lifted him over, the drill instructors said nothing. We had a student cadre of managers, chosen by the drill instructors, whose purpose was to help implement the drill instructor's orders when they weren't present. One day, our student battalion commander directed us to fall out for the morning formation in flight helmets, shorts, and tennis shoes. The drill instructors said nothing. As long as we acted as one, no problem. We were no longer individuals.

Everything was designed for conformity. Our closet and drawer beneath it looked exactly like everyone else's. The closet held our freshly laundered and starched uniforms, all arranged in a precise order. The drawer contained our white T-shirts, boxers, and olive drab socks. A collection was taken, and one of the class officers was allowed to go to town and purchase two-inch-diameter PVC pipes. We cut them into precise lengths. With our underclothes wrapped around them and fitted into the drawers in a specific way, they looked perfect. The socks were rolled individually from the toe, and at the top, the end was turned inside out over the roll. Then, everything was placed in the drawer in a particular way so that every drawer was identical. To further the appearance of perfect uniformity, there was a small cupboard above the closet that was not subject to inspection. This is where we kept our boot polish, brass polish, shaving kit, and all the other stuff that a person needs every day. We kept a few candy bars and snacks in there, too! The Army called snacks pogey bait. The Navy called it geedunk.

Every couple of weeks, there was a formal inspection of our rooms, where we had to be present. With a piece of a wool Army blanket, some Johnson's paste wax, and a buffer kept in a hallway closet, we could make the concrete floors shine! With our rooms perfect and everyone dressed in the Uniform of the Day, as specified on the posted Plan of the Day, each room captain would stand at parade rest outside their door in the hallway, while his roommates stood by their beds. When the inspection party arrived, the room captain would snap to attention and, while saluting, loudly announce that the room was ready for inspection. Nance and I had rooms opposite each other on the second floor. One time, as we were listening to all of the yelling on the first floor, Nance walked over to my room and calmly went to my meticulously made-up bed, reached down, and overturned my mattress onto the floor. My roommates were shocked. After he walked back to his room without saying a word, I walked over and destroyed his closet and dumped his drawer upside down. His roommates couldn't believe it. Bob and I thought it was funny, hurriedly put things back in place, and passed the inspection. We still laugh about that. There are lots of stories about Nance and Moore. Bob says we were famous!

Primary flight school was four months long, with mornings spent studying at a building called the Learning Center and afternoons at the heliport, flying. Book learning was accomplished by using what were called programmed texts. All the student pilots sat in the same classroom but studied individually, quietly learning at their own pace. Flight training was broken down into phases, with the first phase being pre-solo, with each flight having clear goals. Once a particular skill was mastered, the student would move on to the next phase. At the end of every major stage there was the dreaded check ride! If you failed it, you would be given further training until you hopefully passed on your second attempt. If you failed the check ride again, you would likely be sent back to the next class or dropped from flight school. Not everyone graduated. I've taken and given scores of check rides since then.

The programmed texts were short booklets that students would study until they had memorized the required checklists and procedures. They each had up to a dozen items that were required to be memorized exactly. There's no time available while flying a helicopter to pull out a book or written checklist to read the steps. For one thing, it takes continuous use of both hands and both feet to fly one! Flying an airplane, you can cruise along easily without handling the controls constantly. Anyway, when the student felt ready, he would leave his desk and go to the front of the classroom to stand at attention before the instructor

CHAPTER TWO: US ARMY ROTARY WING AVIATOR COURSE

and recite the checklist or list of procedures. The instructor was an experienced pilot who had already been to Vietnam. All pilots use mnemonics to help memorize checklists. Such as the common GUMP check, meaning gas, undercarriage, mixture, and prop. Pilots still use it today. I remember one mnemonic was CIGARBUTTS. Controls, instruments, gas, avionics, runup, etc. Of course, you had to remember several mnemonics.

Flying helicopters in flight is similar to flying an airplane. What sets them apart is hovering. It is one of the most difficult flying skills to master, and because of that, it normally takes several more hours to solo in a helicopter than in an airplane. Before you can take off and fly, you have to be able to hover. I remember the process clearly. The instructor would fly to a large field to allow plenty of space. About the size of a football field or two. There would be others in different areas of the field.

We already knew, from classroom studies, how helicopters work. The pedals control where you're pointing by changing the pitch of the blades on the tail rotor. The stick between your knees is used to tilt the main rotor blades, which controls the direction of aircraft movement. On the left side of the seat is a lever called the collective, which controls the pitch of the main rotor blades, which controls your vertical movement. If that wasn't enough to worry about, on the end of the collective was the throttle, operated like a motorcycle throttle, which controlled the engine rpm. That, in turn, controlled the critical rotor rpm. To top it off, the movement of any control caused a requirement to move every other control! If you push the stick forward to take off, you have to raise the collective to stop the descent. If you raise the collective, you have to add throttle to maintain rpm. If you add collective and throttle, you have to add left pedal to counter the torque. So to maintain a stationary hover, you can't take your hands or feet off the controls for a second because they are constantly moving, making the small corrections necessary for precise control. But just like a child learning to stand, after becoming very skilled through experience, the tiny movements are hardly detectable.

Helicopters, Jets, and Bush Planes

After the instructor pilot demonstrated how to move the controls and pointed the helicopter at a tree or pole on the edge of the field, you were given control of the pedals only and directed to keep the helicopter pointed directly at the pole. This was the easiest skill to learn, especially when the instructor was moving the other controls at the same time. After overcontrolling and swinging the nose back and forth thirty degrees, eventually, you got the hang of it, learning how much to push the pedal and when. The next control the instructor added was the collective and throttle. An army hover is at exactly three feet from the ground to the bottom of the landing skids. At first, the instructor would be on the controls to stop you from bouncing off the ground or climbing straight up to fifty feet. Again, eventually, you got the idea and could keep the helicopter pointing at the pole at approximately three feet.

To put it all together, the stick that controlled the main rotor system was added. It was incredibly difficult to keep the aircraft over a precise spot, with no lateral movement. I saw other guys flailing all over the sky, climbing and descending, backwards and sideways before the instructor took over and quickly put the helicopter back to a three-foot hover. It was pretty funny actually. But once you can hover, it's one of the greatest feelings of accomplishment you will ever have in your life. Very few people can fly a helicopter.

You never forget your first flight. I remember the instructor taking off and climbing to a couple of thousand feet while I observed with total fascination. After a few minutes, he told me to take the controls and not to make any large changes. Then he lit up his cigar and put his foot outside the door and rested it on the landing gear cross tube, his flight suit blowing in the wind. The training helicopters had the doors removed for the Texas heat.

Like all initial flight training, most of the time is spent learning how to take off, fly around the traffic pattern, and land. The first major goal is flying solo, with no instructor aboard telling you what to do. Not only is it a huge confidence booster, but it would now allow the student to go out and practice flying on their own. One day, after a couple of patterns, flying with dozens of other helicopters, my instructor told me

Chapter Two: US Army Rotary Wing Aviator Course

to hover over the grass next to the runway. After I set the helicopter down, he unbuckled, told me to go around twice, and land and pick him up. And leave the landing light on so the tower operator would know that I was a student solo. I soloed with ten hours of instruction, first in my class! I was nineteen.

Each instructor had two students. The students who weren't flying out from the main heliport with the instructor were transported to and from the various practice heliports by bus. There, we would wait in a small building. After the first student finished their lesson, the second student would get in, and after their lesson, they would fly back to the main heliport with the instructor, while the first student would ride the bus back. The heliports were called stage fields, and there were dozens of them scattered across the open country west of Fort Worth, Texas. Different from a regular airport, they had four short, parallel asphalt runways that had four concrete helipads on them. So you made your approach to the closest pad, then, after the helicopter ahead of you hovered forward, you'd move to the next pad. After getting to the furthest pad, you could take off.

After I soloed, while riding the bus back to our base, I noticed the driver pull into the parking lot of a Holiday Inn and park next to the swimming pool. I was carried off the bus by my classmates and tossed into the pool in my flight suit. A tradition for all new solo flyers. Now I could have a wing patch sewn on the front of my hat. And I could fly solo and practice landing in various places using my own judgment, with no instructor.

A critical skill was learning how to evaluate places that would be safe to land in and take off from. Approved solo landing spots were marked with painted tires, placed in various locations in the Texas desert. Initially, you could land at the easy white tire spots. After more dual instruction, you could land at the more difficult yellow tire areas. The red tire spots marked pinnacles and were the most difficult because they were on a small, high piece of ground. After landing, you would friction lock the controls down at idle power and get out and mark the best takeoff spot with rocks. Then you would get back in your helicopter and back up to where the pile of rocks was just in front of you before taking off. The spots would change with the wind, so you couldn't always use the last student's rocks.

At the appropriate time, the student pilots would head back to their home base. There were three types of small training helicopters that the army used—the Hughes TH55, the Bell OH13, and the Hiller OH23. I flew the Hiller. The TH stood for training helicopter, and the OH stood for observation helicopter. Each type had its own base, and there were hundreds of helicopters parked on huge concrete areas. At night, the sky was filled with blinking red lights. There were so many helicopters coming in and out from the heliports that there was no time for talking on the radio. During the day, we followed large panels that were placed in the desert and painted orange. At night, we followed flashing white lights.

The student pilots were called WOCs, which stood for warrant officer candidates. Flight school consisted of about one year of training. Each flight was graded, and your overall scores would determine what type of aircraft you would specialize in. The best students were selected for the most challenging roles, which usually involved flying a more advanced aircraft. One of the graded items at the end of each training flight was "headwork." This would be the instructor's evaluation of the student's decision-making. A passing grade would use a white grade sheet. A failing grade would use a pink grade sheet. Everyone could see when you received the dreaded "pinky." I earned one in the Army.

In primary helicopter training, each instructor had two students. In this case, it was me and Nance. Bob flew first, so the instructor told me to wait in his pickup truck and to run out and take Bob's seat while he kept the helicopter engine running after the one-and-a-half-hour lesson. They didn't allow us much rest in flight school because the drill sergeants would mess with us when we weren't training, so we were always busy. Anyway, I fell asleep during their training flight and had to be awakened by Nance while the IP (instructor pilot) waited, wasting five extra minutes. He was not sympathetic. I was getting a pinky even if I flew like Chuck Yeager!

CHAPTER TWO: US ARMY ROTARY WING AVIATOR COURSE

After completing primary flight training, we were sent to Fort Rucker, Alabama, for advanced training. This training was conducted in the famous UH-1 Huey, built by the Bell Helicopter Company. UH was designated for utility helicopters. This was the aircraft that most of us would fly in Vietnam in a few months. It was much larger than the small training helicopters that we flew in Texas. And they had turbine engines!

I remember traveling from Texas to Alabama with another guy in his 1955 Chevrolet station wagon. We had all of our possessions in the back, with our uniforms on a bar above the back seat. After hundreds of miles and a couple of days, we entered the small town outside the base. About halfway through the town, Greg ran a stop sign that he didn't see. From the passenger seat, I looked to our right and saw a school bus heading right for us. It hit us just behind me, crushing the right rear door and wheel well. After the local police finished with us, we were towed to a shop for some repairs. The right rear wheel wouldn't turn, so the mechanic fired up his cutting torch to remove some of the crumpled metal. As we were watching, smoke started pouring out from a fire that had started. The fire was quickly extinguished, and fortunately, none of our uniforms were burned. We then continued on our way to the base to check in to our new unit. Greg didn't get a ticket. The local population around the Army flight schools was very used to seeing the hundreds of young men who were learning to fly helicopters. Knowing that we were going to war, and seeing the number of Americans killed every day on television, they cut us some slack.

One of the first things warrant officer candidates noticed after reporting to Fort Rucker was that we were treated with a lot more respect by the drill instructors and flight instructors. The goal was not to weed out the slow learners and poor performers now, but to help us complete our training and become professional US Army helicopter pilots who would be going to war in a few months. And knowing that all of us wouldn't be coming back alive. Also, unlike Fort Wolters, we had Saturday afternoons and Sundays off. One of the first things we did was buy a new car. My roommate and I went to the sports car dealership, conveniently located just outside the main gate. The dealerships would let the flight school candidates take a car to try out for a couple of days. They knew we would be getting a big pay raise in a few weeks. My roommate got a black MGB, and I got a tiny 1967 Austin Healey Sprite, white with a black top and red interior. Boy, did we all have fun running around on weekends then. Some guys tried out new Corvettes or Porches.

Soon, we all had girlfriends in the nearby town. And the drill instructors didn't mess with us as much. We could see the end in a few months when we would be Warrant Officers and US Army aviators. The training was intense, with several stages like normal and emergency operations, including many touchdown autorotations, where the engine is not connected to the rotor system, gunnery, night flying, instrument flying, formation flying, and sling loads, which involved moving bulk items by attaching them to a line hanging beneath the helicopter.

Instrument training was especially fun for me, although others struggled with it. The flight was conducted solely by using the instruments to control and navigate the helicopter. We wore a view limiting device, that blocked our view outside of the helicopter. Beginning exercises were performed to build the skills required for precision flying in weather that didn't allow visual contact with the ground, night or day.

One difficult task was partial panel flying, where the primary instruments were covered, simulating failure. An especially hard exercise was performing timed descending or climbing standard rate turns. That meant a 360-degree turn at the standard rate of three degrees per second for two minutes while descending at 500 feet per minute for 1,000 feet at a constant airspeed, using only the basic instruments. This was to develop your scan and concentration, which meant looking at and interpreting each flight instrument while simultaneously making the small control inputs to adjust the rates of turn and descent and continuously moving your eyes from one instrument to the next. While concentrating on interpreting the instrument that you were looking at, your hands were moving the controls to make the corrections for the prior instrument interpretation. The faster you could do that, the

CHAPTER TWO: US ARMY ROTARY WING AVIATOR COURSE

better the results. Partial panel meant failed instruments. So with no attitude indicator, you used the altimeter to stay level. With no heading indicator, you used the magnetic compass to stay straight or turn. Rotor blade pitch controlled the rate of climb or descent. Power was varied to control your speed. For every thirty seconds and 90 degrees of turn, you had to lose 250 feet. Every fifteen seconds, 45 degrees and 125 five feet. Not easy with a compass that leads and lags at varying rates depending on the direction of the turn. But I was pretty good at it and had excellent grades. I would use this skill routinely throughout my career flying jets, props, and helos.

At the end of the instrument phase was a night cross-country flight, to build confidence in our newly acquired skills. With two students flying each Huey helicopter, we were to fly a designated route between several checkpoints that were marked with flares. We would report each checkpoint by radio. The flight was supposed to be conducted in night VFR conditions, meaning that we had good visibility and could see the lights on the ground and city lights in the distance, giving us a horizon. Unfortunately, the weather conditions were not great, but we had a completion date with another class right behind us, so we were going! My stick mate and I soon found ourselves flying in rain, while maintaining our assigned altitude. It was really bad, and we should not have been flying.

All of a sudden, we were IFR, meaning that we could see nothing outside our windshield or anywhere else. We were in the fog! Our instrument training enabled us to fly safely, but without being able to see the ground we were lost and scared. So we decided that we needed to descend until we could see the ground again. I was flying, so I began a descent from our altitude of 1,500 feet. I was concentrating on the instruments, and my copilot was looking out the windscreen for VFR conditions. After descending below 500 feet, and my copilot not seeing anything, I told him to turn on the landing light. As soon as it came on, I saw the tops of trees! We were seconds away from crashing! I quickly pulled the collective up, and the stick back, and climbed back into the clouds. We were soon back in VFR conditions again and somehow managed to find our way back to our base. Many students got lost that night.

When I left for Vietnam in 1968, I let my little brother use my new Austin Healy Sprite. He was just back from the war and didn't have a car yet. While I was gone, he totaled it. Insurance paid me what they thought it was worth, and I continued to make payments on it from my 600-dollar-a-month pay, including my 105-dollar flight pay, and 65-dollar combat pay, until the loan was paid off.

Near the end of flight school, we received escape and survival training. We ate fried grasshoppers and rattlesnakes. Tasted just like chicken. For the final test, in groups of six, just before dark, we were dropped off along a dirt road in the Alabama forest. Each group was given a map, flashlight, matches, a small bag of rice, a little salt, a pot, and a canteen of water. We also got one live chicken or rabbit. My group got a chicken. The goal was to get to one of the checkpoints a few miles away without getting caught by the dozens of drill instructors hiding in the woods. Since we had skipped the evening meal, and to silence the chicken, we decided to eat before proceeding on. One guy grabbed the chicken by its head and started slinging it around until the body flew off. Another guy dumped the rice into the pot with water and put it over a fire that another guy had started. I remember him saying that he would just put all of the salt in since it would probably be good for us! After plucking and dismembering the chicken, it was added to the pot. When it was done, I tried it. It was so salty I couldn't eat it.

So, after cleaning up, we headed out, being as quiet as possible, stopping occasionally to check the map and agree on a direction to go. The riskiest part was crossing a grass runway, where we could easily get caught. Somehow, we managed to cross it without being seen, and after a few hours, made it to the checkpoint. Safe! The reward for not being caught was a ride back to the barracks and a few hours of sleep. Unfortunately, those who were caught, which was most of the class, were taken to a simulated POW camp, where they were blindfolded and bound, put in painful positions, and interrogated by yelling drill instructors for the rest of the night. I heard that a few of

Chapter Two: US Army Rotary Wing Aviator Course

the guys ended up on a paved road, waited for a vehicle to come by, and hitchhiked back.

Later, in Navy flight school, due to having this training, I was the only member of my class to be declared exempt from attending SERE school. It stood for survival, evasion, resistance, and escape. I didn't tell anyone about not having to experience the POW camp. At that time, the SERE training included the use of waterboarding. It was banned in 2007.

I believe that everyone is born with different natural abilities. I don't believe that just anyone who wants to be a famous actor, musician, athlete, or CEO of a company can achieve that simply with hard work. That's ridiculous! The fortunate ones discover, mostly by circumstance, what their abilities are and are also fortunate enough to be able to act on them, meaning supportive parents, with no worries about money for basic needs, resulting in successful careers. I discovered that I was a natural pilot, assuming there is such a thing. It was easy and fun for me. And the US Army was paying for it! Others had to struggle, and some never succeeded. I have been very fortunate.

The graduation ceremony from flight school in February 1968 included a flyover by dozens of Huey helicopters. My younger brother, Paul, a three-striper buck sergeant paratrooper, came from his base at Fort Benning, GA, to pin my bars and wings on. I had my traditional silver dollar ready to hand to the first person to salute me as a new WO-1 "Wobbly One," warrant officer. It was a very special day. Everyone involved was very proud. Even the drill instructors.

Nance's dad had a Cessna 182 in Napa, California, and Bob already had a Private Pilot Certificate. In 1967, you could use your GI Bill money for flight training while still on active duty, which is not allowed now. So Bob suggested that we go to the local airport and get our FAA commercial pilot fixed-wing ratings. Very few army helicopter pilots did that. When we became senior warrant officer candidates, halfway through our year-long training, we could leave the base from noon Saturday until Sunday evening. We found a small flight school with a grass runway, near our base, and started taking lessons. The owner was a designated pilot examiner, and he had a special course for new Army pilots to add a fixed-wing rating to a current pilot certificate. It consisted of ten hours of training and a check ride for 250 bucks. I didn't have it, so I borrowed it from my brother. It was a guaranteed course. In other words, he was going to pass you on the first try! On my check flight, he had to take control and recover from my attempt at a steep turn. I passed, of course, and was now legally allowed to fly people as a commercial pilot for hire. I remember thinking that I would never rent an airplane and fly it without an instructor aboard because I could barely land the plane in calm winds!

So, the day after graduation from Army flight school, we went to the local airport and flew, with a few other pilots, to Atlanta, Georgia, where the FAA General Aviation District Office was located. We were given a special fifty-question written exam, for graduates of the US Army Warrant Officer school. After easily passing the exam, we were issued FAA Commercial Helicopter Pilot Certificates, since the program consisted of a little over the FAA required 200 hours for a commercial license. To get a commercial license in another category of aircraft required only ten hours and a flight test, which we did that afternoon.

Later, when we were getting our multi-engine rating, I was flying at a couple of thousand feet with the instructor in the front, and Bob was in the back seat, waiting for his turn at the controls. The instructor pulled the mixture control on one engine, thus shutting the engine down for a simulated engine failure. One of the emergency checklist items was to turn off the two magneto switches. This is supposed to be done one at a time so that you can be sure that you are turning the switches off for the failed engine. If you mistakenly turned off a switch on the good engine, you would notice a drop in power, but the engine would still be running. I calmly reached up to the overhead panel, located the four magneto switches, and flipped off the two magnetos on the good engine! It was suddenly very quiet, and while the instructor was having a heart attack, I just as calmly flipped the switches back on. The engine hardly had time to slow down and began running normally immediately. After the instructor calmed down, he explained to me that while the switches were off, unburned fuel was collecting in

CHAPTER TWO: US ARMY ROTARY WING AVIATOR COURSE

the cylinders, and suddenly flipping the mag switches on could cause a catastrophic engine explosion. The correct procedure would be to place the throttle at idle and turn the mag switches on one at a time, resulting in an easy engine restart.

Bob and I were now certificated commercial airplane and helicopter pilots and went on to get several more FAA pilot ratings. We are still FAA-certificated flight instructors in both airplanes and helicopters.

Warrant officer candidates were assigned to one of four battalions. They were identified by a colored plastic disc worn under their WOC brass on the front of their caps. Bob and I were green hats, second battalion. My class had hundreds of candidates in it. This was the height of the Vietnam War. In 1968, there were over 500,000 troops in Vietnam. The training was long and intense, but the feeling of accomplishment was amazing. I still remember the first day after graduation, when I wore my US Army officer's uniform, displaying my US Army aviator's wings. Only pilots could wear their flight jackets in place of the dress uniform jackets, so their appearance was unique. I've never been so proud. And to be treated special at such a young age, with my background, was incredible. Being saluted by much older soldiers, some of whom had already been to Vietnam, was humbling.

Everyone was anxious to learn what their next assignment would be, with everyone expecting to go directly to Vietnam as a Huey pilot. I distinctly remember the day that the telephone at the barracks entrance rang and the person who'd called asked for me. I was told that I was going to Hunter Army Airfield to attend AH-1G Cobra School, en route to the Republic of Vietnam. I couldn't believe it! A very small percentage of new pilots would get Cobra training. AH stood for attack helicopter. The Cobra School was at Hunter Army Airfield outside of Savanna, Georgia. The building on the flight line was called Cobra Hall. Hunter AAF was previously a US Air Force Strategic Air Command, or SAC base, so it was built into the ground, half below and half above. There were large concrete parking spaces for B-52s, where a few dozen Cobras were now parked. We got two weeks of Cobra transition training, followed by two weeks of gunnery training. The school trained Army and Marine pilots, who also had Cobras. All Marine Corps, Coast Guard, and Navy pilots wear the same gold wings. Army and Air Force wings are silver, but they differ from each other. I became a rarity, earning both silver Army wings, and later, Navy wings of gold. After graduating, we received thirty days of leave before going to Vietnam.

The Army needed a way to provide protective air cover for the Huey helicopters in Vietnam that were flying soldiers into the field to fight the enemy. They had to slow down to a hover to drop the troops off, making them an easy target. Every Huey had a door gunner on each side. But a special helicopter was needed to carry more firepower. So, the gunship was born.

UH-1 models A and B were originally designed to transport people and cargo. The crew consisted of two pilots, a crew chief, and a door gunner. Some of these older Hueys were fitted with small rocket launchers on the sides, adding fire power to the machine guns fired by the crew chief and gunner. The newer and more powerful UH-1C was much more capable. With a few other modifications, they were called Charlie model gunships. They did not carry troops but fired at targets in the area where the infantrymen were being deployed, by several D model Huey "slicks" flying in close formation.

The Army tasked the Bell Helicopter Company to design a new helicopter specifically for the gunship role. The result was the Huey Cobra. It was narrow, only 36 inches wide, and carried two pilots seated in tandem. The aircraft commander was in the back seat, and the pilot/gunner was in the front. The front seat controls were on the sides, so a sight for the turret weapons could be mounted on the floor, between the pilot's legs. The turret under the aircraft's nose had two weapons, a Gatling gun or minigun and a 40-millimeter grenade launcher. The ammunition for these weapons was stored in a large ammo bay underneath the cockpit and was accessed from doors on both sides of the fuselage. The stub wings carried four rocket pods, or other weapons, that were controlled from the rear seat. With a more powerful engine and a smaller crew, the faster Cobra could lift more weight, translating to more fuel and ammunition. The Cobra was developed quickly, sharing many components with the Huey. Unlike the Huey, the Cobra had air-conditioning!

CHAPTER THREE
Vietnam

(Note: Even though I hear it all the time, I have a hard time saying that anyone volunteered to go to Vietnam or for anything other than joining the military. Some guys didn't even do that. They were drafted. Once you're in, you get paper orders for your next assignment according to the needs of the service. Toward the end of that assignment, you receive orders to your next one. I learned about volunteering early, in boot camp. The drill sergeant announced that we were going on a long march, carrying our field gear, to bivouac for a few days. We would have a 2 1/2-ton truck hauling larger necessary supplies, so he asked for a volunteer with a driver's license. He picked one of the guys with his arm raised, who was thinking he would get out of the marching. The drill sergeant then yelled at him to drive a mop over the barracks floor and dismissed everyone else. Never volunteer!

Another thing I hear frequently is how the military promised lifelong medical benefits. This was supposedly in the contract signed by the volunteer. I don't remember any of that! All I remember is holding up my hand, and after repeating a few words, saying, "I do." I guess the Army and I were married!)

Alpha Company

I arrived in Vietnam in April 1968. It was two months after what was known as TET, the lunar new year in Vietnam when the enemy launched a major offensive. I was twenty years old. My assigned gunship unit didn't have any Cobras yet, so I was temporarily assigned to their sister company, the "Little Bears" for a couple of weeks, to get indoctrinated into the country and the routine of being a combat pilot. I remember being awakened in the early morning darkness by a young enlisted man who worked in Operations, to get ready for our mission for the day. Our living quarters were called "hootches," which were built of wood salvaged from rocket boxes, with concrete floors and tin roofs. The upper half of the exterior walls were screened, since there was no air-conditioning. Each man had a small fan, which was normally passed down from the previous owner, which was directed at your bed so you could sleep in the heat and humidity. I had actually purchased a window air conditioner at Sears to include in my Army shipment to Vietnam. I donated it to our small brick Officer's Club, where we would socialize over a few beers after our missions.

Outside our hootch, there were several "steel pots" or combat helmets that were inverted into cutouts on a wooden shelf. This is where we poured water to shave with. I barely needed to shave, and I tried to grow a mustache to look more mature. To make my new mustache visible, I used my black Kiwi boot polish on it! With no plumbing, we had outhouses. There were two seats inside that were located over the two halves of a 55-gallon drum, placed beneath the seats. Every day, the half drums were pulled out the back, and several gallons of diesel fuel were added to the contents. This was set on fire and resulted in the contents being burned away. You could always see the black smoke coming from the fires. Soldiers were assigned this task for the day. Every base in Vietnam did this, and it resulted in a very recognizable odor which while very distinct, was not particularly repulsive. I would recognize it to this day!

Alpha company had a primary mission of carrying infantry troops into an area where the enemy had been located. The operation was called a combat assault. Before landing the formation of about ten Huey slicks, escorted by two or three gunships, the landing zone or LZ would be prepped by artillery fire. Some areas in Vietnam were within range of up to three separate artillery batteries. Between combat assaults, they flew various missions, commonly called ash and trash. This included supplying troops in the field with more ammunition, exchanging a few troops with others who needed to come in, delivering the Stars and Stripes military newsletter, or delivering holiday meals to the field troops.

The missions that I flew on as a Huey copilot, were mostly "C and C," command and control, flying the ground unit's commander overhead the battlefield to see and direct his troops. It involved hours of circling at a safe altitude—safe but boring. After breakfast, the crew would meet at the helicopter and fly it to a pad at the nearby battalion headquarters and shut down. Eventually, a senior officer and his assistants would come out and board our helicopter. We would fly them to the location where his troops were operating and orbit the area at a couple of thousand feet while the commander observed the situation and directed his forces. Our only break from the monotony was going back to refuel. We did this until the end of the day.

One mission that I will never forget was transporting dead American soldiers. The bodies came from the field in black rubberized bags that had full-length zippers down the middle. They were temporarily stored in steel conex (container express) containers until further transport, eventually arriving in the United States. The heat in the hot steel box would result in a horrendous odor. Several of these body bags were loaded into our Huey to be moved to a central location. I wonder who those young men were. And who they could have become.

Bravo Company

One day, while still with the Little Bears, I saw four brand-new Cobras fly over, and I knew that, as a qualified Cobra pilot, one had my name on it! I was happy and excited when I was told to walk across the dirt road and report to Bravo Company, the gunship company in the 25th Aviation Battalion. That was when I was moved next door to the gunship company known as the "Diamondheads," named for the mountain in Hawaii that was the headquarters of the 25th Infantry Division. I moved into a room whose previous occupant was still in a hospital in Saigon. Another pilot, he was wounded while on a mission during the TET offensive a few weeks before. I was told that the enemy soldiers had overrun the Tan Son Nhut airfield, a major US base located near Saigon, 21 miles south of Cu Chi. And that our gunships were making their firing runs between the main runways.

I was very surprised to see that Robert "Hayne" Moore, was in the same unit and the same hootch! We had gone through flight school together. Hayne had been a senior enlisted man before being accepted to flight school. He introduced me to the dice cup and all of the games associated with it. These leather-covered cups were found in every military club bar in those days. We played for many hours during our downtime. Another hootch mate was George Conger. He was to become my primary copilot. And there was a particularly friendly and happy young pilot, Rich Worthington, whose job was flying one of our small helicopters. Everyone enjoyed having him around.

As in all wars fought by the US in other countries, a lot of the local population was hired to work on the base. We had Vietnamese girls who were called "hootch girls." They would clean our rooms and do our laundry by hand in a concrete-covered common area. They were from the village of Cu Chi just outside the base and would come in every morning along with hundreds of other workers. If we tipped them, they would shine our boots. They didn't speak English, but as always, American soldiers learned how to communicate with a few words and hand signs. All of the soldiers who had them remember their hootch girls. Ours was Lam, pronounced like Lom. She was a very nice young girl. Even though we were occasionally fired at from her town as we flew over.

Within a week, I was flying a Cobra gunship, shooting rockets, grenades, and miniguns at the enemy in support of US troops. We started with one Cobra fire team covering the missions, along with three Huey gunship fire teams. The mission of our unit was close air support, meaning helping the American ground troops that were engaged with the enemy to kill the enemy. This meant firing our rockets, grenades, and miniguns where it would be most effective. Sometimes, that meant shooting within a couple of hundred feet of American troops. A few weeks later, I was selected to be a fire team leader, in charge of two

CHAPTER THREE: Vietnam

Cobra helicopters, and would be making life-or-death decisions affecting many people, most of whom I would never see or know. I had just turned twenty-one. I didn't realize at the time that enemy soldiers were from all walks of life—young single men, older married men with families, professional men, and women. I know now that I surely killed people who were much better human beings than me.

After my year in Vietnam was over and I was back in the States, I learned that Rich had been shot down while piloting a Huey on a "Smokey" mission. All of the crew were killed and only two of their bodies recovered. Rich was not recovered. He's still there. After not finding him, the rescue team was forced to leave because of intense enemy fire. Rich was declared missing in action, and because his body was never recovered, he will always be classified as MIA. He had previously earned a Silver Star Medal, the third-highest decoration for valor in combat, and was on his second voluntary one-year tour. Throughout history, only a small number of soldiers have been awarded the Silver Star. Missing in action American soldiers from all wars is only about 80,000. MIAs from the Vietnam War are currently 1,244.

We were frequently awakened in the night by incoming mortar and rocket fire from the enemy living outside our base. They actually lived underground in tunnels, but we didn't realize that they had a massive tunnel system, some of them right under our base. I learned about it years later from a book, *The Tunnels of Cu Chi*. One of the chapters was about a surgeon who had worked in the underground hospital for years. There were also classrooms, including one that held a US 105mm Howitzer, taken apart piece by piece, carried through the small tunnels, and reassembled underground! About the only thing left of our Cu Chi base today is a popular tourist site featuring a tunnel entrance.

The mortar hitting the ground made a very recognizable "whoomp" sound. The enemy occasionally fired more powerful 122mm rockets, that made a whistling sound when they went overhead. Most of the rockets and mortars were fired during the night, when it was easier for the enemy to remain concealed. After being so rudely awakened, the drill was to roll out of your "rack" onto the concrete floor and crawl out of your hootch to a bunker outside. These were dug into the ground and covered with several layers of sandbags placed on top of steel plates. There was room enough for several people. It wasn't all bad as there was usually a nurse or donut dolly in their nightgowns. There weren't many round eyes in Vietnam!

Once in a while, the enemy got lucky and hit a building or a helicopter. There were a few small shrapnel holes in our hootch. One person was killed by a mortar in the daytime. The mortar landed on the admin building of the Little Bears. A soldier was just sitting at his desk, doing his job. The enemy would target our flight line, and I recall a few instances when mortars landed where our helicopters were parked. Our maintenance hangar was hit one day, with the mortar coming through the roof and damaging a helicopter inside. They were fired from a small opening in the ground, leading to the tunnel complex, all around the base. The entrances were well concealed, and the tunnels were difficult to find and destroy.

All pilots were assigned a secondary job, and mine was to be our unit Cobra armament officer, which was in addition to my pilot duties. There were several options for weapons to be mounted on the aircraft. The nose turret, located under the front pilot's position, and operated by the front seater, was originally configured with a 40mm grenade launcher and a 7.62 caliber minigun. I experimented with putting two miniguns in the turret but eventually went back to the original configuration because, sometimes, the grenade launcher was the best weapon for the task. Options for the four wing mounts, controlled by the aircraft commander in the rear seat, were nineteen-rocket pods, seven-rocket pods, or a minigun pod. There were also options for the rockets and the detonators on the nose of the rocket. We generally carried ten-pound HE or high explosive rockets with a proximity fuse, set to detonate at about ten feet above the ground. We occasionally carried flechette rockets. The warhead contained over a thousand small nails with fins on the back, like tiny steel arrows. When set to detonate hundreds of feet above the ground, the nails spread out over a large area. I can't imagine being hit with those. When the 17-pound warhead rocket came out, equivalent to a 105mm howitzer artillery shell, we

CHAPTER THREE: Vietnam

used them exclusively. The warhead stuck out the front of the rocket tube quite a bit.

My Cobra fire team being rearmed and refueled after a mission.

The aircraft were delivered with a pair of nineteen-rocket pods on the inboard mounts and seven-rocket pods on the outboard mounts. But I figured that you can never have too many rockets! So I chose to configure all of our Cobras with four-nineteen rocket pods, giving the fire team 152 rockets, several thousand rounds of minigun ammunition, and several hundred grenade rounds. I don't see any photos of the Cobra with four nineteen-rocket pods on them. I'm sure that the additional nineteen-rocket pods and 17-pound warheads added hundreds of pounds to the original design weight. I don't remember ever computing, or being concerned about the aircraft's gross weight, and now I think that our aircraft were probably overweight! But it was great having all those rockets to shoot, and no one ever questioned me about it. The Cobra had plenty of power, too. I'm sure I couldn't have done this if our base was in the mountains, as altitude negatively affects aircraft performance.

Helicopters, Jets, and Bush Planes

Since the Cobras were new to our unit, I was the first Cobra armament officer. I was assisted by a senior enlisted man, and we had a building near the helicopters to store and maintain various weapons that could be mounted on the aircraft. I was also responsible for testing and calibrating the weapons after being mounted on the helicopter. This task was fun because the target that I used to make sure the rockets, grenades, and bullets hit where they were supposed to was a crashed airplane, a Douglas A-1 Skyraider, an attack aircraft first used in the Korean War. It was located in a large open field, which meant no cover for the enemy, and it was not too far from our base.

Our base at Cu Chi was located 21 miles northwest of Saigon, and our mission was to provide close air support for the 25th Division AO, or area of operations. This meant that every mission involved shooting, and I don't remember ever coming back without expending all of my ordnance. We had a metal building on the flight line near our helicopters, which we called the "scramble shack," for the four Cobra pilots, or four pilots and four gunners in the case of the Charlie model Huey gunships that were on duty, to hang out or sleep until assigned a mission. During the day, between missions, the guys would nap, play chess, write letters home, or even toss a football outside the building. Some days and nights, we were flying for our entire twelve-hour shift.

Our peace would suddenly be interrupted by the black landline telephone connecting us to our base operations, which would only be used to call us for a fire mission. Three pilots would run to their helicopters and start them up. The lead copilot, who answered the phone, got three critical pieces of information. Radio callsign, frequency, and coordinates. That's all that we needed to know where to go and whom to contact. Then he would run to his helicopter, and off we'd go. The goal was to take no longer than three minutes to get airborne. After informing the fire team leader of the coordinates, as the helicopter was turning toward the battle, the copilot would call for artillery clearance so that we wouldn't get shot down by our own artillery batteries at Cu Chi, as they were constantly firing.

The pilots knew the area well, but we still carried maps because there were no reliable onboard navigation systems in those days. And no land-based navigation aids. At night, it was easy to see where the battle was because there were parachute flares fired by artillery, overhead. Vietnam was a very dark place, with hardly any ground lights. If we ever lost power from our only engine at night, we would surely not survive.

Approaching the target area, maybe ten minutes out, I would contact the ground unit to see what their situation was. When we arrived overhead, after making sure that we knew where all of our troops, which we called 'friendlies', were located, I would formulate a plan for my fire team to fire on the target without endangering any US troops. A fun job! One of the best jobs I've ever had.

One of my first combat missions with the Diamondheads was to fly copilot on our Huey, nicknamed "Smokey." The helicopter was fitted with a fuel tank connected to a ring of perforated metal tubing just outside of the exhaust pipe. When the pilot flipped the switch, allowing diesel fuel into the tubing, it would be sprayed into the hot engine exhaust and would produce a large amount of dense white smoke. This would conceal anything that was on either side of the smoke. There was a downed helicopter in a rice paddy, and the crew was under attack. Our mission was to circle the downed aircraft at ten feet above the ground, flying as fast as we could go, and make a large smoke ring around them in order to allow extraction by another helicopter. Without concealment behind the smoke, the rescue helicopter would surely be shot down also as he landed to pick up the first crew. I received an Air Medal with a "V" device, signifying for valor or heroism. My first combat medal. The highest medal was always awarded to the pilot who was the mission or aircraft commander, with the copilot and any crewmen awarded lesser medals.

On another flight during my first month in B Company, I was flying as copilot on a Huey gunship. The aircraft commander and fire team leader was a captain. From my perspective, he was a senior officer whose decisions were not to be questioned. He was running the show, and I was there to assist, observe, and learn. After he was briefed by the ground commander and identified the friendly positions marked with smoke grenades, he circled around and rolled in for a firing pass. I remember thinking that I would not have chosen to shoot where he was about to. But I said nothing about my concerns, thinking that my lack of experience was not allowing me to see the whole picture. Unfortunately, my initial thought was correct. The captain fired a few pairs of rockets before I heard the ground commander yell ceasefire multiple times. The worst thing that could happen was hitting friendly troops, US soldiers, but that's exactly what happened!

We landed moments later and waited until the wounded men were loaded aboard. I remember seeing the soldiers with bandages covering their wounds, and I couldn't look them in the eyes. We flew them to the 12th Evac Hospital at Cu Chi. A friendly fire incident is taken very seriously in the military, and our unit was grounded for a week while receiving several hours of training on tactics and procedures for unleashing our lethal weapons in the close vicinity of fellow Americans. A major change was made to our rules of engagement. Instead of unleashing multiple rockets at the target on the first firing pass, we would now only fire the first pair of rockets and wait for the ground commander's confirmation of the target before firing again. The first pair of rockets would come from the number one rocket tube, the center tube in the rocket pod. It was to always be loaded with WP, white phosphorus rockets, which produce a bright white smoke on detonation, to allow everyone to see exactly where they hit. We would not fire again until the ground commander confirmed that our rockets were on target, or if not, he would make an adjustment. We never hit friendly troops again.

I was trained to be a Cobra fire team leader by Chief Warrant Officer George Grinnell. George was on his second one-year tour in Vietnam and already had experience as a Charlie model gunship pilot and fire team leader. He volunteered to go back to Vietnam immediately after his first tour ended to be closer to his fiancée, a Chinese girl he'd met in Hong Kong while on R&R, or rest and recreation leave. He studied the difficult Chinese language every day whenever he wasn't flying.

Our two Charlie model Huey gunship teams were Diamondhead one zero and Diamondhead two zero. The two Cobra gunship teams were Diamondhead three zero (George) and Diamondhead five zero

CHAPTER THREE: VIETNAM

(me). I am not certain why there was no four zero team, but I assume it was the call sign of our temporary third Huey fire team, which was not needed after our second Cobra fire team was established. These were also the fire team leader's call signs. So I was the first leader of the newly created Diamondhead five zero fire team.

One team was on three-minute alert in the scramble shack. A secondary fire team was on thirty-minute standby in the company area to replace the primary fire team in the scramble shack, when they were scrambled out on a mission. A third fire team was on the night three-minute alert in the scramble shack. And the fourth team was off. On our day off from our fire team duty, we could hang out at our swimming pool, go shopping at the base exchange, or volunteer to fly other missions, either for a pilot that wanted the day off or flying one of our Hueys, which we did a lot. Because we all liked flying more than anything. We rotated this schedule for the entire year that I was in Vietnam. The shifts were twelve hours long and began at 8:00 a.m. and 8:00 p.m. We would average about one hundred flying hours per month, with a few months requiring approval from the flight surgeon, to be allowed to fly more than 120 hours.

On one of those early missions as a new aircraft commander in charge of the helicopter, but not the fire team, I was flying as George Grinnell's wingman. We were on our way back to Cu Chi when he somehow got the frequency to contact the commander of a fire support base in the area. He asked the commander if he would like us to land on the small temporary base. He said sure, as few soldiers got an opportunity to see a Cobra up close. They saw lots of Hueys; they rode in them. So we did!

In February 1969, my fire team was involved in a major engagement. A ground unit was under heavy attack from hundreds of enemy soldiers. I was about to enter a situation that would have a great impact on my life many years later. The unit was the famous 27th Infantry Regiment, the Wolfhounds. Some of the troops were in the 2nd Battalion, Charlie Company, second platoon, and based at Cu Chi, where I was. Their motto was NO FEAR ON EARTH. On the night shift and sleeping in the scramble shack at the flight line, we were awakened by the telephone, meaning only one thing. Some American soldiers were in trouble and needed help immediately. As usual, the lead copilot, mine, answered the call and got the call sign, frequency, and coordinates. Sleeping in our flight suits, we only needed to run to our gunships, and after strapping in, start them up and take off. We flew at 2,000 feet and 150 knots toward the artillery flares, which were easily visible in the black sky.

By the time I arrived on station with my Cobra fire team, it was well after midnight. The Wolfhounds had already been in contact for hours and had taken many casualties. Second Platoon, Charlie Company had been overrun by the hundreds of North Vietnamese enemy soldiers, who had attacked them under the cover of darkness. As I got closer to the scene of the battle, the enemy began firing 51-caliber anti-aircraft guns at us. In order to see precisely where your bullets are going, the string of cartridges included a tracer shell that glowed red, every several rounds. Fired from our miniguns, they looked like a solid red line that you could walk right to your target. Fired from the enemy anti-aircraft guns, which were much larger and more deadly than our miniguns, coming past our cockpit they looked like flaming footballs . . . and close! I rolled in on the closest gun firing at me and started shooting back. I aimed my rockets at where the enemy tracers were originating, but they kept firing back at the same time. Shooting at them didn't deter them; they were hard to hit and taking them out wasn't my priority. I needed to kill the enemy that were charging the Wolfhounds.

Normally, the two Cobras worked together, flying in a racetrack pattern, alternating making their gun runs. But in this scenario, with three enemy anti-aircraft guns firing at us, I decided that we should make our runs separately. So, I told my wingman, Bob Segers, to stay at 2,000 feet, and I would stay at 1,500 feet or below, enabling us to turn all of our lights off. That way, we couldn't be targeted, except for a few seconds when we were firing and flying at nearly 200 mph. I contacted the second platoon with my FM radio and got the layout. I went first, firing several pairs of rockets, and when I reached the end of my run, at an altitude of about 500 feet, my copilot would cover our climb out

CHAPTER THREE: VIETNAM

with his minigun. After I had expended my ammunition, I would trade places with Bob and wait overhead while he made his gun runs. About an hour or so later, when both helicopters were out of rockets, we headed back to Cu Chi and would normally refuel, rearm, and go back to the scramble shack to await the next mission. I decided to inform our company operations officer that we needed to go back ASAP, which we did. The Wolfhounds needed all the help they could get. We pilots were frustrated that our troops couldn't contact us directly and save all of the wasted time going through proper channels!

All of the Diamondhead pilots at the dedication of a .51 caliber anti-aircraft gun, presented to the unit by the Wolfhounds. They had retrieved it after a fierce battle with the enemy, in which the Diamondhead gunships had received fire from this deadly weapon. The officer on the far left is Major Bert Rice, our Commanding Officer.

By this time, daylight was approaching, so the enemy retreated. My team covered the Wolfhounds as they got their wounded loaded into medical evacuation, or medevac, helicopters and taken to our base hospital, collected their dead, and secured the area. They asked me to check on their LP, or listening post, consisting of a half dozen soldiers in a dugout position located a few hundred yards away from the unit's main camp. They hadn't heard from them since the attack began. I found that the enemy had surprised the soldiers and killed them all. The enemy didn't have time to remove all their dead comrades, as they usually did, and there were more than two hundred of them still on the battlefield. The Wolfhounds had a rough night, and I felt incredibly fortunate, imagining what they had just gone through.

One of the missions that we had was called a sniffer mission. The idea was to find the enemy, even when you couldn't see them beneath the jungle canopy. A special machine that could detect ammonia from urine, in minute quantities, was mounted in a Huey. The sniffer ship would fly at treetop level, and the sniffer operator would read the machine and call out hotspots. A single gunship flying high above and behind would escort the Huey in case it came under fire, and the gunship copilot would make a mark on his map to identify the hotspots. On the way back to base, the copilot would call in the hotspot coordinates to battalion operations so artillery could be directed to shoot at the heavy concentrations, likely indicating where the enemy soldiers were. On one of those missions, I noticed the sniffer ship turning sharply and calling on the radio that they were taking fire and enemy soldiers had been spotted. The crew had thrown a yellow smoke grenade to mark the location. I looked around the smoke and saw two enemy soldiers firing an anti-aircraft gun mounted on a tripod at me. I could clearly see the muzzle flashes as I flipped the switch that armed my rockets and rolled into the fire. At that moment, as I was looking right at them, I heard the 51-caliber bullets hit my left wing less than ten feet from me. I laid down several rockets, obliterating their position, and when I came around again, they were gone. Those 51-caliber bullets made holes you could stick your arm through. Our maintenance officer wasn't happy with me!

The US Army fired millions of artillery shells in Vietnam, and the sound from the big guns was heard around the clock. American soldiers also set up temporary fire support bases—small remote bases, with a few howitzers, to enable units operating away from the large base camps to have artillery support. When I was scrambled to assist the Wolfhounds in February, they were operating from Fire Support Base Diamond One. There were several Diamonds, designated Diamond One, Two, etc., as they were moved to other locations. A couple of months later,

CHAPTER THREE: Vietnam

on the night of April 5th, they called me again. I guess I did a good job the first time. They were under attack, again by a large enemy force, and the Wolfhounds had several dead and wounded. But as before, they had killed dozens of enemy soldiers. I was sure glad that I was flying above the battlefield and was not on the ground, shooting face to face with my enemy. And instead of dealing with the aftermath, I would be flying back to a secure base camp.

There's a thing called target fixation, where you are concentrating so hard on what you're shooting at that you ignore other important things that are going on. Like your altitude! I experienced it twice in Vietnam. The first time, after completing a mission, I was returning to base when I spotted something manmade in the jungle. I descended to take a look and saw several small huts made from bamboo and grass. An enemy camp! I had a few rockets left and didn't see any friendlies around so I decided to destroy it. After rolling in on my gun run, I could barely recognize where the huts were. The camp was very well concealed. So I waited until I could see where to shoot. By the time I could make them out, I was already below 500 feet and should have been breaking off and climbing. Instead, I started firing my rockets. At the last moment, I raised my nose and pulled pitch to the maximum. I barely avoided hitting the tops of the trees! And shooting myself down by flying into my own shrapnel.

Another time, I was trying to knock out a bunker in a tree line that was reinforced with concrete. Unfortunately, I was taking very heavy fire from Viet Cong AK-47s, which my wingman and I failed to notice. On my post-flight inspection after parking back at our flight line in Cu Chi, I found a couple of dozen bullet holes in my gunship. All of these require repair with a riveted metal patch at the minimum. After opening the engine cowling, maintenance discovered other damage that would require depot maintenance level repairs. That meant transporting the helicopter to the other side of the base. The maintenance officer requested that I hover my damaged Cobra along the mile-long runway to the facility. That way, if it came apart, I would only crash from three feet above the ground! Finding no volunteers to ride in the front seat, they put 150 pounds of sandbags in the front and said good luck. It was shaking quite a bit, but I got it there. Fortunately, by that time we had an extra Cobra.

Arriving on station with my fire team one night, I could see that it was a big operation, partly because of all the chatter on the radio. The battleground was illuminated with several aerial flares, and Spooky, an AC-47 gunship, was already at work. The converted passenger airplane, also known as Puff the Magic Dragon, had the seats and windows removed and replaced with miniguns. It could fire many thousands of rounds from multiple guns at once. Very effective and impressive! I was finally able to get in contact with the ground commander and was advised that my fire team would be working the southeast quadrant. Artillery was also being used, and F-105 Thunderchiefs, dropping bombs and napalm. I quickly got the layout, and after briefing my wingman, Bob Segers, I rolled in to lay down my marking rounds. Just after I pulled the trigger, a bright yellow light on my warning and caution panel lit up. I looked down and saw that it was the main rotor chip detector light. It indicated that there were metal chips in my main rotor transmission oil. This meant that the transmission was possibly coming apart and required an immediate landing. Because the radio was so busy, I was unable to contact the ground commander or my wingman. So I just broke off my gun run and flew away from the battlefield.

To find a place to land, I flew at treetop level with my searchlight on. Talk about making yourself a target! Locating a large enough opening in the jungle, I quickly landed, cut the lights off, shut it down, and bailed out. Looking up, I saw Segers orbiting overhead. What a relief. He saw me break off and followed me. Our flare ship was over the battlefield and once again flew over and picked me and George up. I wonder if Segers told the ground commander why we left so suddenly. The next day, when it got light, a large Chinook helicopter from Cu Chi, with a gunship escort, flew to the area and picked up my Cobra, with a cargo hook they attached to the main rotor, and flew it back to our base to get the transmission repaired or replaced.

I had an unusual mission to sink one of the army's river patrol boats that was heavily damaged and had been abandoned by its crew.

CHAPTER THREE: VIETNAM

A ghost ship. They just didn't want the enemy to get anything from it. Blowing it up with rockets was a lot of fun.

Another day, I was given the task of destroying an entire village. The enemy had chased most of the villagers away and taken over their homes. There was even a North Vietnam flag on a pole. I told my wingman to take the opposite side of the main street from me and use his rockets to blow up the hootches. You really couldn't call them houses, but they had been people's homes. We never saw any people, or animals, and the village appeared to have been abandoned fairly recently. The fire control panel in the Cobra had a knob for selecting the inboard or outboard pair of the four rocket pods. Another knob was for selecting how many pairs of rockets each trigger pull would fire. You could select from one to nineteen pairs, and we normally selected one pair at a time. I selected nineteen pairs outboard and pulled the trigger while raising the nose of my aircraft, to disperse thirty-eight rockets into the neighborhood. Then I selected inboard and did it again. So I fired all seventy-six of my rockets on one pass. We then fired all our other ammunition, flew back to Cu Chi to re-arm, and went back again and again, until the village was completely destroyed. We fired several hundred rockets plus many grenades and bullets that day. In retrospect, I wish that we could have waited a few days to see if the villagers would come back. Unfortunately, it wasn't my decision to make.

Following the normal procedure on our way to our target, I contacted the ground forces about ten or fifteen minutes prior to our estimated arrival time to find out what kind of trouble they were in and formulate a plan. On this particular mission, the lieutenant who answered my call was very calm, but after learning what his situation was, I knew that he was in grave danger. His platoon had been on patrol when they were attacked by a much larger force. He said that they were pinned down, surrounded, and running low on ammunition. His radio operator had been killed, along with several others. I asked him to mark his flanks with smoke grenades. He said that he didn't have any flanks, they could see the enemy soldiers firing at them as they were closing in, and to just shoot anywhere around the single plume of purple smoke that was coming out above the thick jungle cover. He told me to shoot as close to the smoke as possible and to not worry about hitting them as they were crouched under some fallen trees. He said that a rescue helicopter was en route and he needed to move his men to a nearby clearing, if they could survive long enough. I decided that in order to give them more time, my wingman and I would only fire a few rockets, grenades, or minigun bursts on each gun run. We did this for as long as we could, but eventually, we ran out of ammunition. I told them that we had nothing else to shoot but that we would continue to make gun runs, hoping that would keep the enemy from advancing so they could try to escape. After doing that for several passes, I told the lieutenant that we were getting low on fuel and had to leave. I felt pretty bad until, after getting back to Cu Chi, I learned that they were safely extracted.

Flying back to base one day after engaging with the enemy, I got a low engine oil pressure light and started losing power. It was a single-ship mission, so I had no wingman with me. I must have taken a round that hit an oil line. So I needed to get on the ground quickly, before the engine failed completely, forcing me to do an autorotation. I'd done dozens of them in flight school, but if not performed perfectly, they could result in major damage to the helicopter. Or me! I spotted an open field, so I lowered the collective and headed toward it. While making a radio call to battalion operations concerning my predicament, I noticed several armed men coming out of the tree line. They could be enemy soldiers. As I rapidly approached the ground and flared the helicopter for landing, thick smoke rushed forward from the engine compartment, engulfing the cockpit. After yelling that we were on fire, my copilot and I shut down and got out as fast as we could. Now, worried about the soldiers, I unholstered my revolver but soon realized that they were friendly US soldiers. Perfect! They guarded us and our Cobra until we were rescued. Another one of my Cobras had to be carried back to base hanging from a cable!

Arriving on station one day, I asked the platoon commander to identify the positions of his troops. It was difficult because they were

CHAPTER THREE: Vietnam

dispersed in elephant grass that was taller than a man and they couldn't see each other. He said that he was trying to direct his medic to a wounded man, so I told him to have the medic pop a smoke grenade. Then have a person with the wounded do the same. As I circled overhead, I could easily see them. I directed the medic to the casualty, and after he got to him, I continued with getting my intended target identified and set up our gun runs.

Another memorable mission was escorting a US Air Force C-130 Hercules transport plane. Their mission was to deliver critical supplies and ammunition to a small outpost that was constantly under fire. A large enemy force had surrounded them weeks ago and was attempting to overrun them. The outpost had a paved runway, but any aircraft that landed would quickly be shot full of holes and stranded there. Besides, the runway was not long enough to ensure safe operations for a heavy transport. So the air force had the crew utilize the LAPES method of delivery—low altitude parachute extraction resupply system. It was used from the sixties through the eighties when it was discontinued. A couple of crashes occurred, resulting in crew deaths, and the method was deemed too risky.

The procedure required the pilot to slow down and lower his landing gear and flaps. Then he would open the cargo door, a large door that opened the entire rear of the plane. It was hinged at the bottom and provided a ramp from the floor of the cargo area to the ground to facilitate easy loading and unloading of cargo, including vehicles. Next, he would make a steep descent to minimize his time at low altitude to arrive five feet above the runway. While keeping his altitude low, the crew would toss a small drogue chute out the back. That would deploy one or more larger parachutes, which would pull a pallet with the cargo on it out. It would drop onto the runway and slide to a stop as the aircraft added power, raised its gear and flaps, and climbed away from the ground while likely taking fire.

After a briefing with the pilot, I told him my plan. I would follow him, and when he was near the runway, begin firing rockets and miniguns at the jungle at the edges of the base, hoping to keep the enemy from firing at him. I told my wingman to take the left side, and I would take the right. That way, we could both fire at the same time, covering the Herc until he was at a safe altitude. The plan worked perfectly and was a lot of fun. Nobody got shot down!

Approaching the area of another mission with friendly forces under attack, I saw several other Cobra gunships in a group. I had never seen that before. After checking in with the ground commander, I was advised to contact one of the pilots who was leading the three other fire teams in the attack on the enemy. The pilot briefed me on the situation and told me to join the racetrack attack pattern they were using. Now there were four fire teams, eight helicopters flying in a large "daisy chain" formation while making gun runs one at a time for multiple trips around the pattern until we expended our ammo and fuel. Talk about fun!

The normal mission was fairly routine. Fly to wherever American troops were in trouble, shoot our rockets, miniguns, and grenades at the enemy, and fly back to our base. If it was a really bad situation, we would refuel, rearm, and go back and do it again. Sometimes all night. So I looked forward to doing something completely different. Like the time when I provided gunship escort for a CH-64 Skycrane, a large heavy-lift helicopter. Only a few were produced, and they were very valuable. A Skycrane had gone down in the jungle, and the second one was trying to retrieve it. Previously, a recovery crew had been flown to the scene and removed the rotor system from the helicopter. This reduction in weight would allow the second helicopter to be able to lift the two parts separately. So the crew attached a cable to the center of the six-blade, 72-foot rotor system and started to lift it. At a couple of hundred feet, I could see a problem developing. The air from the forward motion of the helicopter, added to the air from the downwash of the helicopter, caused the rotor system to start rotating. Faster and faster! The crew of the recovery helicopter had one option. Release it! Any external stores on an aircraft can be released in an emergency by hitting the "pickle switch." I watched it hit the ground and disintegrate. Hundreds of thousands of dollars. War is expensive.

Another unusual mission entailed a special briefing. I was to take my fire team to a classified location and orbit the area as a prisoner exchange took place. It was a good-sized round field surrounded by

CHAPTER THREE: Vietnam

thick jungle. The American side consisted of a couple of NVA (North Vietnamese Army) prisoners and a few US Army escorts. They were to meet a similar group of enemy soldiers escorting American prisoners in the center of the field, leaving simultaneously from positions on opposite sides of the field. After the exchange, both groups would return to their previous positions. I was not to fire on the enemy until both groups had reached their positions on the edge of the jungle. As soon as the enemy group had reached the jungle, I rolled in and unleashed my rockets on them. Strangely, I don't remember any more prisoner exchanges after that!

In Vietnam, there were areas where no one was supposed to be. Around villages especially, if we wanted to shoot at something, we had to get permission from the village chief. That would require contacting our base operations, who would contact battalion operations, who would contact . . . Never mind. But the areas where nobody was supposed to be were called "free-fire zones" and noted on our maps. And we could shoot anyone without asking permission. I always altered my route back to base so that I would fly over the free-fire zones. Because anyone in that area was assumed to be an enemy soldier, carrying messages, or whatever else might aid the enemy and endanger American soldiers. On one of these occasions, I spotted a person running across an open area with a lone tree in the middle. When he saw/heard us, he ran to that tree and tried to hide in a hollow spot in the trunk. Circling around, I could see him trapped there. I should have left him alone, but I didn't. We rolled in on the tree. He didn't have a chance. I regret it now. He didn't even have a weapon.

My best buddy was Hayne Moore. He was a Huey gunship fire team leader. One day, I was flying my Cobra as his wingman. Returning from a mission, we spotted a man on a bicycle in a free-fire zone. Hayne's door gunners fired some rounds at him, and when they came back around, they only saw the bicycle there. They landed and picked up the bicycle and brought it back to Cu Chi. We would use it to ride back and forth to the flight line. Hopefully, it belonged to an enemy courier, and not some hapless farmer. That bicycle would have been equivalent to our family pickup to him. I think I saw a few chicken feathers on it.

Another flight with Hayne ended a little differently. He was flying lead in a Huey gunship, and I was flying wing in my Cobra as he was the senior pilot. On the flight back to base, after the mission, I decided to fly in close formation. Big mistake. It was fine for a while, but I didn't notice how close I'd gotten. It wasn't normal to put two different types of helicopters in the same fire team, and my sight picture was different. But that's no excuse. Suddenly, I heard a loud bang, and it felt like my helicopter exploded. I instantly knew that our overlapping rotor blades had hit each other. By instinct, I reduced the pitch of the blades and checked my instruments. They were vibrating so badly that I couldn't read them. I was falling rapidly toward the ground while transmitting a mayday call on my radio. I was certain that my front-seater, George Conger, and I were about to die. Somehow, we made it nearly to the ground with most of our rotor system still attached. At what I estimated to be between 100 and 200 feet, I pulled the nose up to slow us down. Shortly after that, I pulled the collective control fully up, which added maximum pitch to the rotor blades. We hit the ground and bounced, landing upside down.

We had survived a midair crash in a helicopter. Practically unheard of. Incredible! George got out through his door first. My door, on the opposite side, was against the ground. There was a special "breakout tool" mounted on the top of my instrument panel glare shield. I grabbed it and started breaking the plexiglass canopy to make an opening for me to use. As soon as it was big enough, I climbed out and moved away from the wreckage. Then we waited for one of our Huey helicopters, that heard my mayday call, to pick us up. It was piloted by Bob Segers, who was also a Cobra pilot. I was lucky to be alive. Being at fault, I lost my leadership position for a few weeks because of my poor judgment, but eventually got my Diamondhead 50 fire team back. I was extremely grateful and proud to be one of the fire team leaders—a very select few. And I had many successful and rewarding missions after that. Being in charge of two highly armed and deadly Cobra helicopters was something that I was very good at and enjoyed every minute.

CHAPTER THREE: VIETNAM

Bell AH-1 Cobra helicopter, after being recovered, a day after I crash-landed it in Vietnam. Note the broken rear canopy where I exited.

At Christmas time, our base was visited by Bob Hope and his crew. That year, he brought Anne Margaret with him. I was lucky and was not flying that day. It was a great morale booster for the troops, and of course, unforgettable. During the holidays, the cooks would prepare a turkey dinner with all the trimmings for the troops in the field. We would fly it out to them with one of our D Model Hueys, along with their beer ration.

We had eight active gunships in our unit, four Cobras and four Charlie model Hueys. We also had four small observation helicopters and a couple of standard D model Hueys that were used for various purposes. Sometimes, they were used to deliver supplies to the field troops or transport personnel. One crucial mission was to provide illumination over a battlefield on those black Vietnam nights. This was done with either artillery flares or a Huey that we called a flare ship. I could usually see where the battle was by spotting the parachute flares in the distance. The flares would be stacked on the floor of the Huey, and the lighter would be triggered as it was tossed out the door by a lanyard attached to the helicopter. Another aviation company had a flare light off inside their Huey. The white-hot magnesium produced two million candlepower of light for three minutes. It was so bright and hot that the crew couldn't get near it to kick it out the door. It melted through the floor, which contained the flight controls. The crash killed all aboard. After that, our company devised a solution. A 55-gallon steel drum was cut in half lengthwise, and the two halves were mounted on their sides outside the helicopter, providing two containers for the flares. So, if one was inadvertently lit before being tossed over, the entire container could be released. Occasionally, while flying, we would see a burned-out flare under a 16-foot parachute go by out of the corner of our eyes. Hitting one would have been deadly!

Another use for the D model was for a Firefly mission. Again, American ingenuity designed a very bright lighting system using seven landing lights from a C-123 transport airplane, mounted in a cluster inside a Huey. This could be directed by the crewmen to light up potential targets for the gunships. Once we tried dropping mortar rounds from a Huey. We also had our maintenance team fabricate a steel carrier for a 50-caliber machine gun and mount it in one of our D models.

One of the Charlie model gunship pilots was very religious. His name was David Stock, and we called him "Preacher." On Sundays, when a ship was available and he was not on duty, he would fly anyone who wanted to go, to another base to attend services. I never thought of it before, but maybe he was preaching!

Because we only served in one unit of dozens spread across the country, we didn't know about the many ways that other units were using and modifying their Hueys. Some pilots volunteered to go back to Vietnam a second time and would likely be in a different unit. A rare few went back a third time. I generally always had a plan for future adventures and different experiences. Been there, done that, so I was in no rush to return. Also, you can avoid the grim reaper only for so long.

Every unit in Vietnam had a commissioned officer whose job it was to forward recommendations for combat awards. I never knew who our awards officer was. No one ever talked about awards or med-

CHAPTER THREE: VIETNAM

als. Many years after flying in Vietnam, after I had gone back into the Navy after college, a senior officer made a comment about my Silver Stars. Then I started noticing how rare they are. In Vietnam we would learn that we were to receive an award when, standing in formation, the commanding officer would stop in front of you and pin it on. My combat medals include two Silver Star awards, one Bronze Star, and an Air Medal with a V device, indicating valor or heroism. All aircrewmen were authorized to be awarded one Air Medal for every twenty-five missions. I was awarded eleven Air Medals for my first six months in Vietnam. Although I earned approximately twenty Air Medals over the year I was in Vietnam, I was never awarded any more. I assumed that it was just too much paperwork to spend so much time sending them in. Besides, how many do you need? I had already left Vietnam for the States when I got one award, so it was forwarded to my new assignment. I was handed a large envelope one morning while briefing my student pilot. I opened it and found my second Silver Star. Medals, by regulation, are supposed to be awarded at an appropriate ceremony. I didn't show it to anyone. Just took it home. I always thought it was probably a fairly common award, but I've since learned that they are not. In my twenty years of active military service, I never saw anyone else wearing one. My research shows that less than 150,000 Silver Stars have been awarded, many of them multiple awards to one person. That's out of millions of soldiers who served in combat.

Near the end of my one-year tour in Vietnam, I was concentrating on training my replacements, Greg Bucy and Bob Segers, in the art of being fire team leaders. They were both excellent pilots and natural leaders, so I felt good knowing that my fire team would be in good hands. A few Cobra pilots returning from Vietnam, would receive orders to the Cobra helicopter school, known as Cobra Hall, at Hunter Army Airfield near Savanna, Georgia, to be an instructor pilot, teaching pilots in the Cobra before they went to Vietnam, like I had done a year earlier. The main difference for me was flying in the front seat as the aircraft commander. I had to demonstrate each maneuver using the short controls on the sides of the seat. The left control was the collective, a short handle with the throttle on it. A turbine engine runs at 100 percent rpm, so once you set full throttle, the control is only moved up and down to control the pitch of the main rotor blades. On the right side was the cyclic control, which tilted the rotor system in the direction that you wanted to move. Not coming up from the floor, it was very short, and therefore, required little movement to get the desired response. (Several jet fighter aircraft have side controls, as well as civilian jets). These side controls are in addition to the tail rotor control pedals that you press with your feet. Because of having hundreds of hours of experience in the Cobra, it quickly became natural to fly from the front seat. In Vietnam, we only flew from the front seat en route while in cruise flight, never when taking off or landing, which are much more precise maneuvers.

```
                        DEPARTMENT OF THE ARMY
                   HEADQUARTERS, 25TH INFANTRY DIVISION
                        APO San Francisco  96225

      GENERAL ORDERS                                  16 March 1969
      NUMBER    3378

                        AWARD OF THE SILVER STAR

      1.  TC 320.  The following AWARD is announced.

      MOORE, CHARLES D.  W3159164              CW2  USA
      Co B, 25th Avn Bn, 25th Inf Div
      Awarded:  Silver Star
      Date action:  25 February 1969
      Theater:  Republic of Vietnam
      Reason:   For gallantry in action:  Chief Warrant Officer Moore distinguished
                himself by heroic actions on 25 February 1969, while serving as an
                Aircraft Commander with Company B, 25th Aviation Battalion in the
                Republic of Vietnam.  When Fire Support Base Diamond came under
                enemy assault, Warrant Officer Moore volunteered to fly a mission
                in support of the beleaguered ground element.  Upon arriving at the
                area under attack, Warrant Officer Moore was informed of the tacti-
                cal situation.  Realizing the consequences of accurate enemy 51
                caliber machine gun fire, Warrant Officer Moore, with complete dis-
                regard for his own safety, flew his aircraft at tree top level in
                order to detect enemy movement.  Exposed to deadly hostile fire,
                Warrant Officer Moore placed devastating mini-gun and rocket fire
                on the aggressors.  He continued to concentrate his fire on the
                automatic weapons positions, enabling other gunships to fire on the
                advancing enemy ground troops.  His valorous actions contributed
                immeasurably to the repulsion of the insurgents and success of the
                mission.  Warrant Officer Moore's personal bravery, aggressiveness,
                and devotion to duty are in keeping with the highest traditions of
                the military service and reflect great credit upon himself, his
                unit, the 25th Infantry Division, and the United States Army.
      Authority:  By direction of the President under the provisions of the Act of
                Congress, approved 9 July 1918, AR 672-5-1, and USARV Reg 672-1.

      FOR THE COMMANDER:

            OFFICIAL:                            ROBERT L. FAIR
                                                 Colonel, GS
                                                 Chief of Staff

            W. F. VAUGHT
            LTC, AGC
            Adjutant General
```

One of my Silver Star award citations.

CHAPTER FOUR
After Vietnam

Bob Nance got orders from Vietnam to be an instrument instructor pilot at the same base I was assigned to, Hunter Army Airfield, next to Savannah, Georgia. So, naturally, we got an apartment together, a couple of lava lamps, and started chasing girls! 20 July 1969 was a Saturday, so we were both off. We set up our 35mm cameras from Vietnam, on our tripods in front of the television and watched Neil Armstrong walk on the moon. Incredible!

In Vietnam, one of the Cobra crew chiefs, Salvatore Ambrosio, was from Long Island, NY. He had an uncle there who owned a large car dealership. So he ordered a new Z28 Camaro, silver with black racing stripes, and I ordered a new SS396 Chevelle, with all the options, in a beautiful blue. Both were 4-speeds. After Bob got home, he bought a new SS Camaro. It was 1969, and life was good! Most guys, while still in Vietnam, purchased nice cameras, huge reel-to-reel tape decks, and large speakers. We bought them at the base exchange in Cu Chi. When I went on R&R in Hong Kong, the first day there, I went to a music store with several long-playing recording tapes that I had previously bought. I made a deal with them to fill them up with current American popular music and I would pick them up at the end of the week. I had blank tapes from a couple of buddies, too. I had two tailored suits made and bought some nice jewelry. The Seiko watch I bought had an alarm with a tiny clapper in it. After winding it up, I would put it in a glass ashtray to make it louder. One of the rings I bought was gold, with a large Lindy star sapphire. I later had it made into a ring for my mother.

Instructing at the Cobra school was fun and was the beginning of my lifelong passion for teaching others how to be better pilots. We briefed our students at 5:00 a.m. and were finished by noon. Except for the night flying phase, of course. The month-long course was separated by two weeks of Cobra transition training and two weeks of gunnery training. During the first two weeks, the emphasis was on normal maneuvers and emergency procedures. The second two weeks were spent at the gunnery range, learning how to utilize the weapons systems on the Cobra.

All through flight school in the various helicopters we were trained in, we were required to be able to land safely without engine power. Even though a helicopter has the glide ratio of a hammer, in some situations it is safer to land without engine power than an airplane. One advantage is that you don't have enough time before reaching the ground to get scared! But the main advantage is that you can dissipate most of your energy vertically and stop in a very small area. An airplane must dissipate its energy horizontally, requiring a large area to completely stop. During the deceleration phase, the energy is being absorbed by the ground, trees, buildings, or water. We practiced doing autorotations by rolling the throttle to idle so that it provided no power to the rotor system. Immediately after losing engine power, the pilot must lower the collective fully to reduce the pitch of the rotor blades before any rotor rpm is lost. Of course, that would cause an extremely high sink rate and little time to reach the ground. The air forced up through the rotor system would keep the blades turning at normal rpms. As I recall, the desired air speed during the descent was 70 knots, about the same as a training helicopter today. At 150 feet, we would raise the nose to slow to a minimum forward speed, and at 50 feet, start raising the collective control, adding pitch to the rotor blades and slowing the descent, to touch down gently with little forward movement. That was the idea anyway. These were always done to a touchdown and complete stop. Then we would roll the throttle back up to full power, raise the collective, and take off. Many helicopter pilots today never do a touchdown

CHAPTER FOUR: After Vietnam

autorotation, except in an emergency. Too risky. Many practice autos were resulting in accidents.

Between the base and the gunnery range several miles west was a railroad track. We flew at 400 feet on the right, or north side going out and on the south side coming back, day or night. One day, I was flying back when I heard someone call mayday, mayday, mayday. I looked over and saw another Cobra on the other side of the track spinning and going down. I yanked the stick to my left and headed straight toward him. I watched as he descended and crashed. The helicopter slammed into the ground and was completely destroyed and burning. Obviously, there would be no survivors. There was nothing I could do to help them, so I circled overhead and directed the emergency helicopter to our location. The investigation found that the tail rotor had failed, and the vibrations caused the tail rotor gearbox to separate from the aircraft. This changed the center of gravity by such a large amount that it could not be counteracted, so the main rotor blades likely hit the tail boom.

The instructor pilot had gone through flight school with me and Bob over two years before. He was recognized early on as a leader and was our student battalion commander. I remember his father, who was a colonel, pinning Benny's bars and wings on at graduation. From then on, every Cobra preflight included a special inspection of the tail rotor system. Over my flying career, I witnessed many fatal crashes. These pilots were two young men with most of their lives ahead of them, one with a young family and just barely home from Vietnam and the other who was getting ready to go.

Another friend whom Bob and I had gone through flight school with was Ed Shanahan. He also crashed his Cobra while instructing at the Cobra school, killing him and his student. They had hit a tree while climbing out of a confined area, possibly after an aborted practice engine out approach. Sometimes, flying can be dangerous.

A military tradition at the time called for the student pilot to gift his instructor with a bottle of his choice upon graduation. If you were a beer drinker, you could get a case of beer. In Vietnam, we would get a bottle from the crew chief if the rotor blades stopped perfectly crosswise. If they stopped perfectly aligned with the fuselage of the helicopter, the pilot had to gift him one. I would occasionally make a wager with my pilot student that I could put a pair of rockets in a small lake, located about a mile or two down range. Since I had no rocket sight in the front seat, he would take the bet every time. What he didn't realize was, as he was firing rockets with everything set perfectly, I would mark a small x on the windscreen with my grease pencil. I never missed!

Besides demonstrating how to safely fly the Cobra inverted, I showed my students how critical the vertical trim was when firing rockets. The correct power setting was 30 inches of torque, which made the rocket fly to your aiming point. If you had too much power, more than 30 inches, the rocket would climb above your aiming point, going long, because it would be forced into the relative wind. After putting the aircraft into an autorotation, with the low power and torque setting causing a rapid descent, I would point the nose well above the horizon, pointing my weapons toward the city several miles away. The rockets would come out of the tubes and immediately plunge toward the ground, detonating safety below us.

Bob and I started building and racing model airplanes. The ones that we had were controlled by sixty foot-long wires that were attached to the airplane's control surfaces on one end and then to a handle for the pilot on the other end. They were called U-Control planes. After crashing a few planes that we had spent hours building, we discovered a two-plane kit called the T-Square. It was a simple design with no landing gear, and using an iron on plastic covering, could be built in an evening. It was a lot of fun standing back to back and trying to cut the ten-foot crepe paper streamer tied to the tail of your adversary. After we ran out of fuel, we would land, refuel, and go again. Eventually, one of us would get a little too aggressive and hit the other guy's plane.

As you know now, midair collisions usually end in a crash. Ours always did! So we would collect the pieces, put them in a pile, squirt some airplane fuel on them, and light them. This was after salvaging the engines and controls, which we would use later on our new T-Squares.

CHAPTER FIVE
COLLEGE

One morning in 1970, after I had been there a year and a half, all instructor pilots were told to go to the auditorium that was in Cobra Hall. There, it was announced that we were being separated from the Army six months earlier than the date on our orders. The war was winding down, and the Army would have way more helicopter pilots than they needed. A few of us were offered commissions as first lieutenants if we extended our commitment to stay in the Army and make it a career. It would also mean a fixed wing aircraft transition and another tour in Vietnam. I chose to get out and move on to the next adventure and turned down the offer. So, a few months later I put all of my belongings in my 1969 Chevelle and drove to California. Mom was still in college, and I had no particular place to go, so I headed to Napa to stay with Bob, who was already back home, until I figured out what I wanted to do. I eventually got an apartment in Redlands, CA, and worked at a gas station while attending San Bernardino Valley College. I took physics and a few other courses but mostly let my hair grow and chased girls. I also joined the flying club, where our student advisor was Art Scholl, a famous aerobatic pilot at that time. He was known for the Lomcevak maneuver, where you flip your aircraft end over end. He did this in his Dehavilland Chipmunk. After the end of his routine, as he taxied in front of the crowd, he would slide the canopy back and put his little dog, Aileron, up on his shoulder or on the wing for the people to see!

Helicopters, Jets, and Bush Planes

One day, I saw a full-page advertisement in a flying magazine about a college in Florida that had a large flight school, Florida Institute of Technology. The degree program that interested me was Bachelor of Science in Air Commerce, with courses like airport design, aviation history, technical writing, and others that related to aviation. The computer course was passenger and freight forecasting. Chemistry was fuels, oils, and lubricants. The elective courses were flying courses that resulted in obtaining a pilot certificate or ratings in various categories. I had lots of those! So I applied and included copies of my pilot certificates. By taking a heavy course load, with the credits for my pilot certificates and going year-round, I could graduate in two years. I had some GI Bill money left, and I could instruct the other students at the flight school. Then, even with four years in the Army and two years in college, I would still be under the maximum age of twenty-six, to get accepted to the Air Force or Navy flight schools and learn to fly jets.

I quit my job and headed east, stopping in Las Vegas for a couple of days. While checking in at Caesar's Palace, I noticed a lot of people showing up for the entertainment and asked who was performing. It was Elvis Presley. Missed it. It was sold out anyway.

Several days later, I arrived in Melbourne, Florida, where the school was located. I found an apartment for seventy-five dollars a month, upstairs in a little old, converted house. I saw the owner mowing the yard one day and offered to do the job. He cut ten dollars off the rent every month. I painted the old claw foot bathtub orange. Always did like bright colors. I got a job at the nearby Sears store as a tire salesman at the auto center. I was on commission but did very well. School was fun as most of the professors were retired military officers. There were even a few ex-army helicopter pilots attending. I was taking up to twenty-four units per quarter, so my life was school, work, study every day for two years.

I met a young guy named Jim, who had started flying right after high school and was a DC-3 pilot for a large real estate company in Florida. I think he was only nineteen. He was flying another DC-3 from Pittsburgh to Van Nuys, California, for a company that was relocating there, and he needed a copilot. I jumped at the opportunity and

CHAPTER FIVE: College

got approved to miss classes and work for a week. I wasn't qualified in the airplane, so I rode in the copilot seat and read checklists and raised and lowered the landing gear and flaps. That was really fun, flying across America just above the Rocky Mountains in clear skies and mild temperatures. After landing at various small airports for fuel, we would slide our cockpit windows open and stick our elbows out. I had long hair and wore mirrored sunglasses and a black leather motorcycle jacket. Two young guys must have made people wonder as the DC-3 was able to carry many bales of marijuana!

When we arrived at Van Nuys, we were given instructions to hold near the airport until some World War II fighter planes took off. There were a lot of them—part of the reason that Van Nuys Airport was always one of the busiest general aviation airports in the world. We finally got permission to land, and after parking the plane, started checking the place out. Pilots are alike in their passion for flying and airplanes, and they want to fly them all. We saw a P-51 WW2 fighter getting ready to go flying. Jim noticed that it had been fitted with a rear seat, so he asked the pilot if he could get a ride. Jim paid a hundred dollars for his share of the fuel and hopped in. Every pilot's dream! I didn't have the money to spend. While waiting, I watched a commercial being filmed in a nearby hangar for a new flying car. There were two adults sitting in the front seats and two children in the back seats. They were filmed while looking out the windows, pretending they were looking at the ground. A company had removed the twin tail from a Cessna Skymaster and fitted it to the back of a Ford Pinto car. After landing, you would detach it and leave it at the airport. It was all painted to match and looked great. Unfortunately, both the prototypes crashed, killing the two inventors, so that was the end of that project.

During my second year of school, a new Sears store manager decided that I wasn't needed, so I looked for a new part-time job. I actually took a full-time job for a while. There was a Piper Aircraft Company plant about forty-five minutes south of Melbourne, in Vero Beach. Four of us students decided to apply for jobs there and were hired. We worked from 11:00 p.m. until 7:00 a.m. and attended classes during the day. We all had different jobs. Mine was installing engine cowlings, propellers, and landing gear doors. We were given a list of tools to purchase for our particular job. Most of the several tools could be found at Sears. Any other tools needed could be checked out from the tool room in the plant. It was fun. Most people don't know that, unlike cars and trucks, airplanes were hand-assembled in those days, and a lot of the components were custom fitted to each one. In my case, the cowlings needed to be trimmed to fit individual planes, and I did that with an air-powered angle grinder. I ruined more than a few while learning how to do it. One guy's job was fitting the single cabin door. Not only did this require some precision cutting but a lot of shaping with special hammers and dollies.

One perk of the job allowed those of us with pilot certificates to fly the newly built aircraft. They wanted a few hours on the airplanes before delivering them, to find any problems. The aircraft were various single-engine models and a new twin-engine model. They all had the new air-conditioning system. The single-engine, four-place Cherokee 140 was only four dollars per hour, including fuel!

My best friend, Neal Chancellor, worked with me. He was from Key West. His father was the sheriff, and he lived on one of the many manmade canals with a dock and a boat. On weekends, we would fly one of the planes there and go catch a bunch of lobsters for dinner. A few miles out by boat, the water was less than 20 feet deep and crystal clear! Equipment was a gunnysack, gloves, mask, snorkel and fins, and a wet mop with most of the strings cut off. If we couldn't see enough of the lobster to grab with our hands, we would shove the mop into his hideout, twist it a couple of times, and pull him out. Then, we would rip the tail off and put it in the gunnysack. People had placed old car hoods on the bottom, and after lifting one end, we would find several lobsters under it. There were also structures built way out there that were called shacks. They were small and square with one side open, covered platforms on stilts. We would hang out there, and some people camped on them. Years later, I learned that the environmental movement had resulted in the dozens of shacks being removed.

CHAPTER FIVE: College

I only worked at the Piper plant for one quarter of school, but at least one of the guys quit school and worked there until retirement. I went back to flight instructing between classes and on weekends. Several of the students were recruited from wealthy areas of the northeast. One of my young students had what was probably his mom's car, like a Lincoln sedan. One day, I was walking past the car and found that he'd left it running with the air-conditioning on, of course. The flying lesson would take two hours! He had long hair and tried to go flying in flip-flops, but I made him get some shoes. He was a good pilot, though.

One day, the chief pilot of the flight school, who was twenty-seven years old, asked me to fly him and his wife to watch the launch of Apollo 17. I guess he didn't want to concentrate on doing the flying himself. They rode in the back seat and I was alone in the front seat. I circled around a couple of thousand feet over the Indian River just south of Cape Canaveral. I think it was around midnight and very dark when the Saturn Five's huge and powerful rocket engines fired, launching Commander Eugene Cernan and his crew off into deep space to make the sixth and final landing on the moon, over fifty years ago. The launch was very impressive and memorable. I didn't realize it at the time, and many other times in my life, that I was chosen for this role because of the confidence that others had in me.

Flying across Florida with a student one day, I saw something large in the sky several miles away. We flew over to investigate and found the Goodyear blimp going to some event. Another time, at the flight line before going flying, several of us were watching the dean of the school, who was an older pilot, taking off. He was flying an executive DC-3, one of several aircraft that had been donated to the school. Soon after becoming airborne, he turned sharply toward us, passing overhead at a very low altitude, obviously not normal. We learned later that he had taken off with the external control locks on and did not have much control. Somehow, he landed at another airport and took them off.

Occasionally, I would have a weekend or holiday off. One weekend, I did a parachute jump. Along with several other guys, I learned how to do a PLF parachute landing fall after you hit the ground. The modern civilian sport parachute is rectangular, allowing much more control and a stand-up landing. We were using round parachutes like the US Army still uses today. First, we strapped on our main chute, which was in the back, and the reserve chute was in the front. These were surplus military chutes with a 28-foot diameter canopy. There were two lines that ran from opposite sides of the canopy to the jumper, and they had toggles that could be pulled down individually, collapsing an edge of the canopy to give some control over the direction you were pointing. Also, when within 20 feet of the ground, you would pull both toggles fully down, which would reduce your descent speed. We were also equipped with a radio so the instructor could give us directions.

We all got into the back of a Cessna 182, which took off and climbed to a couple thousand feet, and one at a time, stepped out of the opening where the door used to be. Grabbing onto the wing strut and standing on the tire while the pilot stepped on the brake, we let go. As instructed, when we were safely away from the plane and stabilized, we pulled the ripcord, which released the canopy into the relative wind. The feeling was incredible. I looked up at the canopy, and I swear it looked like an umbrella up there. I looked at the ground, and everything was so tiny that I could barely see the cars and people. Due to being in the moving air mass, there was zero wind, so sound carried far. I heard people talking and dogs barking. It seemed like I was suspended in the sky, with nothing moving. That was about to change! Approaching the ground in a large, open cow pasture, I appeared to fall faster and faster. When I thought the time was right, I pulled both toggles and readied myself for the PLF. It all happened very fast but seemed to work out pretty well. Except the part where you jump to your feet and run to your canopy so you could collapse it completely and gather it up. Unfortunately, the day that we jumped was very windy. We could hardly get to our feet to catch the canopy because it was dragging us through cow pies! We all survived and had a great experience.

PART TWO

1974–1992
Ages Twenty-Seven to Forty Five

CHAPTER SIX
NAVY LIFE

Halfway through my senior year of college, in 1973, I applied for the US Air Force and US Navy flight programs. The Air Force accepted me for a class beginning a year later. The Navy accepted me for a class beginning in a few months. I chose the Navy. While waiting for my orders to arrive, I drove to my grandparents' home in West Virginia. As a backup plan, I applied to fly Hueys for the Ohio National Guard. I was accepted, but days later, I received my orders for the Navy. My family wanted me to stay, of course, but I wanted to fly jets.

So I was soon off to Pensacola, Florida, to begin the year-and-a-half-long process of completing my second military flight school. After a few months of officer training there, we would be commissioned as ensigns and proceed to flight training at another base. I would be an older student, called a candidate, with a lot of pilot ratings, and experience flying small airplanes and helicopters, which none of the others had. But I would still be treated like everyone else, even after the year of being a candidate in the Army while completing boot camp and flight school. AOCS, or Aviation Officer Candidate School, was sixteen weeks long, and would be followed by flight school.

The first two weeks were pretty intense, physically as well as mentally, with drill instructors yelling at us at all hours of the day, even in the early morning darkness when running outside after being awakened

CHAPTER SIX: NAVY LIFE

ten minutes earlier for PT, or physical training. This phase was called indoctrination or indoc, with no book learning or flight training but a lot of physical training and marching. We had to meet a certain standard, and when we ran the obstacle course or other courses, they were timed. All this was very similar to the Army boot camp.

On Sunday morning, at the end of the chaotic first week with hardly a moment's rest, we were marched to the chapel. No drill instructors accompanied us inside. What a relief! After the pastor finished his multi-denominational sermon, he told us to relax, before opening a newspaper and reading the headlines and sports scores. Then he announced that he was open to questions about what lay ahead. This was because most of us had very little knowledge about the officer and flight programs that we were involved in. The naval recruiters knew even less or were sworn to secrecy. After several questions were answered, he asked if anyone had ever been an officer in the military before. A few of us raised our hands. He said that we were lucky because, following the next and final week of indoc, we would receive no additional military training, like marching and sword drills, and would be moved to a separate building from the others, where we would maintain a room but were free to get an apartment off base! I had never heard of this before; it was a well-kept secret. What a great surprise. I still had to pass all of the physical tests like the obstacle course, swimming, running, and various other activities; otherwise, I just showed up at the classroom for the academics to learn about things like seamanship, naval leadership, military history, naval warfare, etc.

At the end of the two weeks of indoc, one day, everyone was ordered to gather all of their belongings in a large basket and form up in the street outside the barracks. The plan was to march us to our assigned training battalion, where we were to move into our new barracks. While standing in formation in front of the headquarters building, holding our baskets prior to marching out, I heard someone yell through an open window, for number fifty-six, me, to fall out and report to the commanding officer's office inside. I ran into the building and knocked the requisite five times on his door. On hearing the word "enter," I stepped inside to salute the young captain, who was changing out of his uniform to his street clothes in preparation for riding his Harley motorcycle home. He immediately said, "Relax, sit down, your military training is over." I was in shock after the intense past two weeks. What a feeling! It took a while to sink in that in his eyes, I was a fellow officer and not a lowly candidate like I had been thirty seconds ago!

He told me that I was going to move into a separate barracks with the few other prior military officers. We would maintain our quarters in a ready-for-inspection condition but could move into town and only report to the base for the scheduled academic training and physical training tests. We were never inspected or harassed again. The chaplain wasn't joking.

The swimming training was conducted at one of the two Olympic-size swimming pools. They were inside buildings and were called training tanks. We had a civilian instructor, Mr. Martin, and no drill instructors were present. He addressed us as we sat in bleachers at the side of the pool, explaining the kinds of training we would receive over the next several weeks. He looked us over, and of the three dozen candidates, pointed at three individuals. I was one of them. He said that we would have to work extra hard to meet the requirements because we would not float! Mr. Martin had been a swimming instructor for thirty years and could tell from looking at our bodies, and he was absolutely right. I was a good swimmer but always knew that I could not lie on my back and float like most people. I could walk across the bottom of the pool! While all of the other guys played and joked around in the pool, I worked to keep my head above water. So the underwater swim, mile swim, drown proofing, and many other things that we were going to be tested on were a challenge for me. Did I mention that all the training and testing was done in flight suits and helmets?

One test was to escape from a mock-up of a helicopter fuselage that you were strapped into. This simulated escaping an aircraft that had crashed into the water. It was affectionately called the Dilbert Dunker. It was mounted on the side of the pool, and after everyone was inside, it was flipped upside down into the pool. Talk about being disoriented. Being blindfolded certainly didn't help! There were two

CHAPTER SIX: NAVY LIFE

safety divers underwater to help the guys who couldn't find their way out. They would have to try again.

Another day, we all boarded a few small boats and went out into Pensacola Bay. While the boat was underway, each of us would take turns standing on a platform on the back of the boat, in flight gear of course. We also wore torso harnesses, worn by ejection seat equipped aircraft pilots. They were used for carrying the pilot's survival equipment, and for attaching them to the ejection seat. The instructor would attach the harness to two straps with quick-release fittings, and then, we would jump into the water. This exercise was called the parachute drag, simulating being dragged by the wind after ejecting over water. While being dragged through the water, we would have to get on our back, and when given a signal, find the release fittings by each shoulder and pull them simultaneously, releasing us from the parachute. Free of the straps, we would swim to an inflatable raft and struggle aboard. When it was full, we would be taken to shore. We were given cups of hot soup while shivering from the winter cold water. Lots of fun and games!

Another exercise was called the burning oil swim. One of the dangers of flying off an aircraft carrier might involve a crewman who ends up in the water finding himself surrounded by burning fuel. The technique to escape this predicament is to move the flames away from your face by quickly moving your hands back and forth, taking a breath of air, and swimming underwater until you needed air again or got away from the fire. Mr. Martin told us that they first tried to do this training by actually pouring diesel fuel into the pool and lighting it! But it was too difficult to clean up afterward.

So, after a few months, at a formal ceremony, I was commissioned an ensign in the United States Navy. Now I would go through the Navy's flight school as an officer and not a candidate like I was in the Army's flight school. That meant living off base and driving to work every day like regular people do. What a concept!

The next several weeks were spent soloing and flying the T-34 Mentor at the various practice fields around the Pensacola Naval Air Station. Military aircraft types were designated according to their mission. For example, T was for training aircraft or squadrons, A for attack, F for fighter. The T-34 was a tandem-seat version of the Beech Bonanza airplane, but fully aerobatic. Soloing is the first milestone a pilot achieves in his career. I was already an experienced pilot and flight instructor, so all of this was easy and fun for me. On arriving at a practice field, the procedure was to join the traffic circle, which was a left-hand circular pattern around the field, and slide the canopy of the tandem-seat aircraft back, in preparation for landing. I felt like a WWII pilot! We were also introduced to aerobatic maneuvers like loops, rolls, Hammerheads, Immelmann turns, Split-S, half Cuban eight, precision spins, and more.

CHAPTER SEVEN
Naval Aviation Schools Command Flight School

Upon graduation, students were assigned to the type of aircraft they would fly in the fleet according to their grades in the T-34. Not everyone could be a fighter pilot. The major divisions were called pipelines. The three initial pipelines were jets, props, or helos. I easily got my first choice of jets. There were three jet schools, and I was assigned to Kingsville, Texas. The primary jet trainer was the North American T-2 Buckeye, a tandem-seat, straight-wing, twin-engine aircraft.

The first day of jet school, I met Charles "Choo-Choo" White. He collected model electric trains and had rooms full of them, hence the nickname. Everyone was wearing the normal khaki uniforms instead of flight suits because this was orientation day. I was his first student since being transferred from his F-4 Phantom squadron to the Naval Aviation Schools Command. He noticed my Army pilot wings and several rows of ribbons, the combat awards on top. After chatting awhile, I could tell this was going to be fun.

The T-2 was really easy to fly, smooth and fast. On your solo flight, the instructor would fly another jet alongside. Lt White had me fly inverted while he joined my wing and took a picture. I don't think that was in the lesson plan! We flew together for the next several months while completing the different stages of training, just like the Army.

Except in the T-2 the instructor flew in the back seat and the student flew from the front seat. For instrument training, the front cockpit had a curtain that blocked all outside view. Simulating poor visibility in weather, we learned to fly strictly by instruments. Of course, I already knew how to do this and really enjoyed it.

One day, after arriving at the end of my instrument approach at Corpus Christi Naval Air Station, about a hundred feet above the runway, Lt White told me that he had control of the aircraft and to pull the curtain back. He was about to show me something else that wasn't in the lesson plan! Then he added full throttle while descending to 50 feet, and at the end of the runway, at 250 knots, he pulled straight up to end up inverted over the runway at several hundred feet. After multiple aileron rolls, we departed for our base. So this is how we fly in the US Navy! Cool.

It took about half an hour to get back to Kingsville and land. After taxiing to our parking spot, a couple of military police cars pulled up beside us. The base where Lt White had performed his impromptu air show was where the admiral was based and he either saw us or was informed about it. A call to the tower identified us, and another call to our squadron commander was the result. The MPs took Lt White directly to the BOQ or bachelor officer's quarters, where he was confined during off-duty hours for the next week. His wife and children would come and visit him in the evenings. We both learned a lesson that day!

I guess I wasn't getting enough flying, so I bought my first airplane, a 1938 Piper J-3 Cub. Recently rebuilt and painted in the original bright yellow color, it had a more powerful engine installed, enhancing its performance. Like the original, it had no electrical system, which meant no starter, radios, or lights. One cool feature was the single split door that allowed the upper half to be latched to the bottom of the wing and the lower half to rest against the side of the fuselage. Due to the Texas heat, I always flew with it open. For starting, the pilot, if alone, would stand outside the cockpit, behind the propeller, where he could reach the throttle with one hand and the prop with the other. Then, with the magneto switch on, he would flip the prop over until the engine started. Kingsville was named after the nearby King Ranch.

CHAPTER SEVEN: NAVAL AVIATION SCHOOLS COMMAND FLIGHT SCHOOL

Initially, it was a million acres. I chased a lot of cattle in my little J-3! I would land on a dirt road when I needed a break. One of the instructor pilots had a similar plane, and we would fly formation and play fighter planes and try to get behind the other guy. We even tossed a roll of toilet paper out and tried to chop it up on the way down. The Cub was fun to spin, and I also liked doing loops and barrel rolls with it.

After completing primary jet training, I transferred to the squadron next door for advanced jet training in the TA-4 Skyhawk, a two-seat training version of the A-4 that was used in Vietnam. It had a single engine and a swept wing, and its performance was similar to the advanced tactical jets flying from the carriers. It was a lot faster than the T-2 and the swept wing allowed for a roll rate of 720 degrees per second, like the F-4 Phantom that I would fly next. Several months of day and night flights, including formation, instruments, gunnery, cross country, aerial refueling, and lots of ACM, air combat maneuvering, which used to be called dog fighting. The final phase, like in the T-2, was carrier quals or qualifications, consisting of arrested landings and catapult launches, day and night.

Prior to every new assignment, Navy officers would submit their "dream sheet," listing their top three choices for their next job, in order of preference. We called the official form a dream sheet because you were assigned according to the needs of the Navy. Sometimes, they didn't exactly match. The next pipelines for jet pilots were fighter, attack, or anti-submarine. My first choice was fighters, and I received orders to Fighter Country USA at Oceana Naval Air Station in Virginia. The squadron was VF-101, the Grim Reapers. They were responsible for training all of the new F-4 pilots on the East Coast. I was matched up with a newly minted naval flight officer or NFO, Tom Holston, who was a required aircrew member but not a pilot. He would be my back seater during our training. His duties were communications, navigation, and weapons systems management. In fighters, he would become a RIO, radar intercept officer. Using his radar, he could direct the pilot by giving him various commands to control the proper intercept heading, speed, and altitude in any weather conditions. That's what all-weather fighter means—we don't have to see the enemy to shoot him down. In clear weather, the pilot would maneuver against the enemy as necessary to get the advantage and shoot him down, with the RIO scanning the skies with radar and visually for any other threat. The Air Force called their backseaters GIBs, guy in back.

The Phantom was the first jet that I ever flew with afterburners, so the first flight was in the rear seat, with an instructor in the front, doing the flying. The next flight, we switched seats, and I was in the front seat with the only flight controls. After that, Tom and I flew together. On take off, after lining up on the runway, you advanced the throttles to the first stop or gate, which is one hundred percent, or military power. After checking all of your engine gauges, you move the throttles around the gate, or notch, to the afterburner range. This adds large amounts of fuel to the exhaust system, producing much more thrust and acceleration. I pushed them full forward to maximum afterburner. When they light off, you get a definite kick forward and accelerate rapidly. At the proper speed, you pull the stick back to lift off, immediately raise the landing gear and flaps, and pull the throttles out of afterburner to conserve fuel.

In the early seventies, the rules were more relaxed. I remember when married pilots were allowed to take their wives on a high-speed run down the runway. They weren't allowed to lift off, but I'm sure the afterburner ride was quite a thrill. I should have been allowed to take a girlfriend! I also remember doing section take offs, where the two jets lined up on the runway in formation and pushed the throttles forward at the same time, and lifting off in formation. Landing in formation was equally fun. I felt like a Blue Angel! Those maneuvers aren't allowed now.

I purchased a townhouse in Virginia Beach, and Tom and I moved in. He had a yellow Porche 911, and I had a red Corvette. We spent a lot of money on whiskey and women. The rest we just wasted! I also had my J-3 Cub. One weekend, I flew it to Kill Devil Hills, NC, where the Wright brothers first flew. I followed the beach at a low altitude. I went there to learn to fly hang gliders. The course mostly consisted of running from the top of a sand dune and then gliding down to the beach several times.

CHAPTER SEVEN: NAVAL AVIATION SCHOOLS COMMAND FLIGHT SCHOOL

Earlier, I related how I earned my first pink slip when learning to fly helicopters in the Army. The second one was in the Navy, in VF-101. I was flying one of three F-4 Phantoms with my RIO, Tom, in the back seat. The training mission was to practice tactics that a "section," which was two aircraft working as a team, would use against a single enemy aircraft. So we would call it a 2v1 (two versus one) scenario. The single lead aircraft would be flown by the instructor. So I was assigned the right side of the lead F-4, and the other F-4 would stay on the left side. That way, we wouldn't have to worry about where the other guy was to avoid any conflicts. En route to the training area and back would be in a three-plane formation, with me on the right wing and my section mate on the left wing. After a successful one-hour training flight, it was time to head back to Miramar Naval Air Station. We would join up in a "running" rendezvous, where the lead aircraft flies a straight line toward the airport and the other aircraft have to catch up and smoothly move into position, 20 feet below and behind the leader's wing. All Navy tactical aircraft use the same procedures, including the Blue Angels. It is very precise flying, but we were well trained, and it's a very standard procedure.

Anyway, I noticed as I was getting closer when approaching the leader that my rate of closure was a little fast, a lot fast! The normal way to slow down was to raise your wing, but then, I wouldn't be able to see the leader very well as he would be under my wing. So, in a split second, I made the decision to do a "canopy roll," which is not taught in flight school, but I was confident that I could do it. I'd heard about it. When close to the other aircraft, you pull up slightly and roll over the top of the other aircraft so that your canopies are in full view of each other and you're looking into each other's cockpit, about 50 feet apart until you get on the other side, where you complete the 360-degree roll, ending up in the wingman position on the other side. Unfortunately, that was my section mate's side, but fortunately, he hadn't arrived yet. The instructor in the lead plane yelled over the radio, "Would the Blue Angel get back on his side of the formation." Automatic pinky. Very satisfying, though. I bet it looked amazing!

Helicopters, Jets, and Bush Planes

Later, in my fleet squadron on another training flight in the Phantom, the objective was to practice section tactics against a single dissimilar aircraft. I was flying as wingman with an F-4 piloted by Garry Weigand, nicknamed "Wags," a Mig killer who had shot down a Mig-17 in Vietnam. The pilot of the dissimilar aircraft, an F-14 Tomcat, was Vance Parker, whose previous pilot assignment was with the Blue Angels. We had a successful flight and joined up for the return flight to Miramar, Wags on the left wing and me on the right. We flew a tight formation so we would look good coming into the overhead break. We had many sayings in naval aviation. One was, "Better to look good than be good."

There was actually a very practical reason for this entry. As practice for arriving at the aircraft carrier at sea. It gave each aircraft the proper interval for completing the arrested landing and to taxi out of the landing area, with very little wasted time as everything involving flight operations was time-critical. Arriving overhead the ship or base, the normal procedure was for each aircraft to do a hard left 90-degree roll five seconds apart, beginning with the left wingman, then the lead, then the right wingman, me. When Wags broke left, the lead suddenly rolled into me, and I instinctively rolled away to avoid contact. We were flying just a few feet apart, so there was no room for error. Then I saw a piece of Wag's wing falling off his airplane. I realized that his wing had hit the tail of the lead plane, bumping up underneath it and causing the right roll. I immediately left my position and followed Wags as he entered a downwind position for landing. I flew close to him and assessed the damage. It was not bad enough to call for an ejection, so he kept his speed up and landed as I followed closely. So Wags and Vance, like me, had survived a midair collision. He and I were members of an extremely small group. In the Phantom, you can't see your swept wings as they are behind you, and the F14 tail is very large, so Wag's wing was under the F-14's tail. Maintenance did a quick repair, and we left for a seven-month cruise to the South China Sea a few weeks later. I don't know how they kept that one quiet!

After several months of training in the F-4, including ACM (air combat maneuvering) and day and night carrier landings, everyone

CHAPTER SEVEN: NAVAL AVIATION SCHOOLS...

was looking forward to seeing what fighter squadron they were going to be assigned to. There were F-4 training bases on both US coasts, and normally, you would be assigned to a squadron on the same coast where you trained. The squadrons on the East Coast would deploy aboard ships that would patrol the Mediterranean Sea, while the squadrons on the West Coast would deploy aboard carriers that would patrol the western Pacific Ocean. One day, it was announced that the Navy needed another crew in California. Tom and I jumped the highest and got orders to VF-191, "the Hellcats," at Miramar Naval Air Station, known as Fightertown USA, in San Diego. And we thought Virginia Beach was fun! It was the summer of 1976.

Tom sold his Porche, so he drove my Corvette, and I flew my J-3 Piper Cub across the country. My little sister was having marriage problems, so we agreed to meet at her house in Greenville, Mississippi. To prepare the J-3 Cub for the long cross-country trip, I had a wing fuel tank installed and connected to the small nose tank just behind the engine. Then I had a friend weld a fitting into the bottom of a ten-gallon metal barrel, which I connected to the three-way fitting on the nose tank. The barrel was strapped into the front seat, as the J-3 is flown solo from the back seat. I bought a small motorcycle battery and an electric fuel pump from the auto store and connected them with a lamp cord with a switch on it. That way, after the wing tank was empty, and the nose tank had room for more fuel, I could flip the switch on and transfer from the little barrel in the front seat. With the three tanks, I could fly all day without stopping. Now I had a West Virginia hillbilly fuel transfer system! Worked great.

To plan the 2,300-mile flight, I went to the chart room at the squadron. Of course, this was before anyone invented GPS, and with no navigation radio, I planned to use the old-fashioned navigation system called pilotage. That's one of the first things that we learned in flight training—how to look at the ground below and instantly relate it to what you see on the chart. That way, you could fly along the line that you had previously drawn on it marking your route. Taping several navigation charts together, after laying them out on the floor, I drew a straight line on them and cut the 20 feet of charts down to a foot wide or so, then folded them like an accordion. I had no radio or lights, so I would fly all day, land at an airport with no control tower, and hitchhike to town. No problem. Except when I got to Greenville. The chart showed that it was an uncontrolled airport, but now they had a control tower! I saw a man mowing his yard. It looked big enough to land in, so I landed. I was going to ask him to call the airport and tell them that I didn't have a radio and was coming in. The man was not very happy about me landing in his yard. He yelled, "What the hell are you doing?" So I yelled back over the engine noise and took off. The procedure for communicating with no radio is very simple. The tower has what's called a light gun, which they can point at an aircraft, and by flashing red, green, or white lights, tell the pilot what to do. The pilot is supposed to circle to the left until he gets a green light to land. I got a green light, so after tying my plane down, I went up to talk to the controller. Even though the light signals are meant to be used in an emergency, I arranged to fly in and out for the next few days, so that I could give my sister and her two little boys rides. The small airport was not very busy, so it was not a problem. Plus, it gave the tower controllers practice using the light gun. My sister and I decided that she would fly to California with her sons after I got a house for us, and Tom and I departed.

CHAPTER EIGHT
Arriving in California and Aircraft Carrier Operations

I found a house to rent near the base in Poway, California, and Tom and I got familiar with our new squadron. In those days, all the bases had different social clubs for the lower ranks like petty officers, middle ranks like chief petty officers, and upper ranks like warrant officers and commissioned officers. O'Club membership was mandatory, so all of the pilots and NFOs were members. The clubs all have a dining room and large multipurpose rooms, but for us young, single pilots, the only room we cared about was the bar! During our almost two years of flight training, we had little time for entertainment, so after joining our new squadron, we had to make up for lost time. Friday night happy hour was the highlight of the week, and we all had a lot of fun together. We didn't have any female pilots in the Navy yet, but local girls were allowed to enter the base to go to the O'Club. In fact, for formal events, they were bussed in!

    I remember my first dinner at the O'Club. I was seated at a table with my date and another couple. The chairs were on casters. People were dancing, when all of a sudden the William Tell Overture started playing. Everyone around us started heading for the dance floor, while still sitting in their chairs! So we joined in, propelling our chairs forward by pulling with our feet. Like the Flintstones car! We were all going in a big circle around the dance floor. What a blast!

Helicopters, Jets, and Bush Planes

Bars have house rules, and the military aviator bars had a lot of them. If you entered the bar with your cover (cap) on, the bartender would ring the brass bell hanging over the end of the bar, requiring you to buy a round for the house, meaning everyone. This would only happen once to the offender as he would never forget it. If the bar was full it could be very expensive. Whenever the bell was rung, everyone erupted in cheers, knowing that a free drink was coming. If you ever stepped behind the bar, the bell was rung. If you wanted to celebrate a promotion or graduation, you could walk up to the bar and ring the bell yourself, buying everyone a drink. Some rules required you to buy everyone in the house drinks, others required you to only buy the customers sitting at the bar drinks. These were just a few of the rules.

Then there was the dice cup. When several of your squadron mates arrived and sat down together at the bar, someone immediately asked the bartender for a dice cup. The bar kept several of the leather cups, with five dice in them, under the bar. Starting at one end of the group, the dice were shaken, then dumped out onto the bar in a loud fashion, by slamming the open end of the cup down onto the bar. Aces, with one dot, were wild, and after selecting the dice that you wanted to hold, the remaining dice were placed back in the cup, shaken, and slammed down again. This was repeated until you were satisfied with your hand. Then the dice were placed back in the cup and passed to the guy beside you. After everyone had a turn, the highest hand was out and didn't have to roll again. This continued back and forth between the ends of the group, until the last two players. After they rolled, the last man left had to buy the round of drinks. Another rule was that the first guy out had to order the next round before the last hand was played. If he forgot, he also had to buy a round! I forgot a couple of times. I was a slow learner.

We spent the next few months preparing for our deployment of seven months aboard the USS *Coral Sea* aircraft carrier. The cruise was known as WESTPAC 77 for the western Pacific and 1977. The commanding officer of my fighter squadron, VF-191, was Denny

CHAPTER EIGHT: NAVAL AVIATION SCHOOLS...

Moore, who had been a North Vietnam prisoner of war for eight years. He was released in 1973, four years before. My executive officer was Jim Ruliffson, whose previous assignment was as commanding officer of Topgun, Naval Fighter Weapons School, located across from our hangar at Miramar Naval Air Station, in San Diego, California. I was assigned to be his wingman. Before departing the States, and after all of the air wing squadrons were aboard, the carrier engaged in the required pre-deployment evaluations, called workups. Its purpose was to ensure that all of our ship's complex systems were in top condition, and to practice flight operations with the air wing until all of the various elements involved were working together seamlessly and performing safely.

US Army pilot wings and US Navy pilot wings, with a photograph of the USS Coral Sea aircraft carrier.

During this period, one of our F4 Phantoms crashed into the sea. All flight deck operations are filmed and are also watched live on monitors throughout the ship. The pilot was our wing standardization officer, Slick Burns, and his RIO was Mark Checchio, one of my squadron mates. The shipboard camera showed the aircraft losing power on one engine during its catapult launch. Without both engines operating in full afterburner, the F4 could not accelerate fast enough to fly at that critical stage. The Navy diver on the rescue helicopter immediately jumped into the water and saved Mark. In the background, Slick appeared to be struggling and waving one arm around. By the time the diver reached Slick, he was gone. Being ejected after Mark, he was closer to the water, and maybe a piece of the aircraft had hit him. So just before leaving the States for several months, we attended a memorial service at the base chapel, along with Slick's wife and children. A flyover formation of Phantoms, with the missing man position empty, was emotional for us all.

Chuck Moore, ready to get a catapult shot off the USS Coral Sea aircraft carrier, in the Western Pacific in 1977.

CHAPTER EIGHT: Arriving in California and Aircraft...

Commander Ruliffson, nicknamed Ruff, liked to give the troops a little show when we came back from a mission. So he would ask the air boss, who was a senior officer in charge of aircraft operations on the flight deck, if we could hold overhead and be the last planes to land. The boss would announce to everyone on the flight deck via loudspeaker that the last jets to come aboard would be doing a low-level, high-speed flyover. So everyone was watching. I would slide behind the lead plane into the "slot" position like the number four Blue Angel. I flew very close and could only see the two big exhaust pipes of the Phantom 20 feet in front and 20 feet above me. It took total concentration, and I could not look away for even a second, so I had no idea where the ship, water, or anything else was. We were going about 350 mph. I was told that we flew very fast and low over the flight deck, pulled up, and did a roll or two before separating and coming back to land. Probably looked pretty cool. It was really fun. If only we'd had smartphones then!

I was very fortunate to be in this squadron. I was scheduled to go to Topgun, but with all of the training required before deployment, due to everyone being together for only a few weeks, there was not enough time. What had happened was our ship, the *Coral Sea*, was not supposed to make another cruise but go inactive due to its age. However, the replacement ship wasn't quite ready, so on very short notice, the Navy decided to make one more last cruise of the *Coral Sea*. The previous Air Wing had been disbanded, and the fighter jets, the F-8 Crusaders, were flown to the boneyard, the aircraft salvage base in Arizona. So volunteers like Tom and me were put together for one cruise. After the cruise ended, our squadron was disbanded, and we all went to different squadrons.

Halfway through our seven-month deployment we got a new executive officer, who had been a senior department head. It was Rod Knudsen, another eight-year North Vietnam prisoner of war. With our top-secret clearance, we were allowed to read any of the prisoner-of-war debriefs. Rod was a Phantom backseater, a RIO, when he was shot down. After ejecting and being injured from that, he got on the ground okay but spotted North Vietnamese civilians coming to take him prisoner. There would be a large reward given to them for capturing an American flyer. Hoping to evade capture, Rod pulled out his .38 and shot a couple of them. But they got him tied up, threw him into the back of a pickup truck, and drove him to the nearest military base several hours away. Rod was the first POW to be tortured. Refusing to give the enemy anything other than his name, rank, and serial number, in accordance with the Geneva Conventions, he was beaten severely. After the POWs were released eight years later, they were asked what they wanted to do next. Rod said that he wanted to go to flight school and become a pilot. So he was a new F-4 pilot like me, even though he was our executive officer, who would normally be a very experienced pilot. But having been in combat, flying in a Phantom before, he knew everything that I didn't know.

Our home base while on deployment was Naval Air Station Cubi Point, Philippines, located at the edge of Naval Base Subic Bay, on the island of Luzon, the largest and most populous of the seven thousand islands. The small town outside the base was Olongapo, and it had a main street with about a hundred bars and thousands of bar girls. I thought I was in heaven! What a town. Things were cheap for Americans, and the San Miguel beer was excellent. Probably a lot like the Wild West towns like Dodge City, Kansas in America a hundred years before. Or Dawson, in the Yukon during the Gold Rush of 1899!

Access to the town from the base was via a short bridge across a heavily polluted river that everyone called the shit river, with good reason. There were always several wooden canoes tied up on the side of the bridge, about ten feet below the walkway. In each canoe was a few young girls, dressed in white, trying to get the attention of the sailors walking into town. Most of the sailors would toss them a peso, or some other change, which would land in their canoe. Incredibly, some boys, probably under ten years old, would be swimming in the river, also trying to entice someone to throw them a peso, worth two American cents. The most famous was Henry, because he wore a US sailor's round, white hat, called a dixie cup, with his name in black magic marker on the front. You could toss a peso into the filthy brown water in the dim evening light, and he would dive under the surface to retrieve it. Henry always came back up with his peso! I suspect that there was more than one Henry because he was always there and he never grew up.

CHAPTER EIGHT: ARRIVING IN CALIFORNIA AND AIRCRAFT...

During my deployment, I was selected to shoot down a drone, simulating an enemy aircraft, twice. It was for training purposes and very controlled with strict rules of engagement. So we received a half-day briefing on the scenario and the procedures to be followed. The drone had a flare on a wingtip that my heat-seeking missile would hit, blowing the wing off the drone. The rest of the drone would descend on a parachute, to be recovered and used again, because they were very expensive. The drone was extremely maneuverable as it was light, powerful and strong, capable of several g-forces, and it was a challenge to get behind it and shoot it down. My RIO would locate it on our radar and then direct me to it in a precise intercept procedure.

A pair (called a section), of Fighter Squadron VF-191 F-4 Phantoms, over Southern California in 1977, before deploying to the Western Pacific aboard the USS Coral Sea aircraft carrier. They are flying in close formation, with the leader in front and the wingman flying a few feet away.

Once we got within visual range of it, after several minutes of hard maneuvering, I could get behind it and listen for a steady tone in my headset telling me that my missile had acquired and locked onto the target and was ready to be fired. A trigger on my stick launched the missile from my wing, and we would watch it head for the drone. Again, we had been briefed on the very precise procedures to perform prior to pulling the trigger. After getting into position with a steady tone in our headsets, we were supposed to tell the drone operator that we had a tone and were ready to fire. The operator would then put the drone in a hard turn, which we couldn't match, before saying, "You are cleared to fire." Then I could shoot, and because of the drone's hard turn, my missile would head for the flare that was burning on the drone's wingtip and either miss or explode, destroying the wing. I had a better idea, of course. Pull the trigger just before saying "ready to fire." The result was that my missile went into the exhaust pipe of the drone and destroyed it! It was really cool. It's only money. Maybe it was an old drone anyway.

Fighter planes are flying weapons platforms, so they don't have a lot of space for radios and fuel tanks. So we basically had one communications radio and one navigation radio. If we were to fly alone, in weather that didn't allow us to see the ground, and have a radio failure, we'd be in serious trouble. For safety in the case of a failure, we always flew in pairs, called a section in the Navy. A four-plane flight, like the Blue Angels use, is called a division. Anyway, we were always concerned about fuel. We had to be conservative about the use of afterburners for that reason. If you took off in afterburner and left the throttles at max burner, your engines would consume the 2,000 gallons of jet fuel and flame out in under ten minutes! We always went straight to the overhead tanker after the catapult shot to top off our tanks. The tanker was a modified A-6 jet from our carrier.

A tanker was always circling overhead the ship when flight operations were being conducted. It was fun joining up with it and was especially challenging at night. After the cat shot and raising the gear and flaps, staying at full throttle, I would level off at a few hundred feet above the water and accelerate until reaching a point five miles from the ship, the radius around the ship that the tanker flew. At that point, I was doing close to 400 knots. I knew that the tanker was at 10,000 feet, flying in a standard rendezvous turn, a left-hand circle at 250 knots in a 30-degree bank. So next, I would pull up sharply, producing several Gs, into a vertical climb, and watch the altimeter wind up fast. A few seconds later, passing through about 8,000 feet, I would pull the stick back to be inverted and level at the same altitude as the tanker. As

CHAPTER EIGHT: ARRIVING IN CALIFORNIA AND AIRCRAFT...

soon as I, or my RIO, spotted it, I would point my jet at him and join up. At night, all that was visible were the navigation lights, small red and green lights on the wingtips and a small white light on the top of the tail. All aircraft have a rotating red anti-collision light on the top of the fuselage. The one on the tanker aircraft was changed to a green one to help identify him. His call sign was Texaco.

If one aircraft had a communications radio or navigation system failure, he could be led back to the carrier while flying on the wing of the other jet. Communications with your wingman were always accomplished when flying in formation, using hand signals in daylight and a flashlight at night. This was also done to prevent an enemy from listening on our frequency and gathering information about our operations and procedures. When flying in close formation, we could see each other easily in the daytime and the flashlight at night. We did a lot of formation flying, and tanking, getting more fuel from a tanker aircraft. The Air Force uses large land-based transport aircraft for tankers, but due to operating aircraft carriers far out at sea all over the world, the Navy used tactical shipboard aircraft modified to carry a hose and other equipment to deliver fuel to other aircraft. Pilots would join up in formation with the tanker, and after communicating using hand signals, maneuver to a position directly behind and slightly below.

The end of the refueling hose had what was called a basket that was a couple of feet wide at the opening. It resembled a big badminton birdie and had tiny lights around the opening for nighttime. In the F-4, the pilot would activate a switch, extending his refueling probe from the right side of the aircraft. Maintaining the proper sight picture, the pilot would slowly move his aircraft forward, and at the last moment, he would see the probe, hopefully entering the basket and connecting. The flying was extremely precise, and the probe would frequently just miss the target. With no more than a couple of tries and a little coaching from your RIO, you were successful. After getting your fuel, you would back out and move to the other side of the tanker to watch your wingman do the same. After he was refueled, he would retract his probe and slide his aircraft underneath yours, arriving on your outboard wing

Helicopters, Jets, and Bush Planes

in formation. Then you would head off to accomplish your mission. The entire process could be done without talking on the radio.

You were expected to follow directions from the combat information center, located below the flight deck on the ship. At first, it was uncomfortable watching your fuel gauge go down after being sent away from the ship to intercept a simulated enemy aircraft, knowing that you didn't have enough fuel to make it back. But what you didn't know was that the controller had already dispatched a tanker to meet you on the way back. Professionalism and trust. No sweat.

An aircraft carrier is designed for continuous operations, meaning that with half of the aircraft on the flight deck and half on the hangar deck, one deck below, after launching the airplanes off the flight deck, you can move all of the aircraft on the hangar deck up to the flight deck. It took fifteen minutes to launch the aircraft from the flight deck. Then an hour to move the aircraft on the hangar deck to the flight deck and refuel them and fifteen minutes to launch them. Now the first launch is returning, and it takes another fifteen minutes to recover them. That means that the carrier operated on an hour-and-a-half cycle, and this could be maintained continuously. The other ships in the task force had the mission of protecting the carrier or replenishing stores of food, fuel, and ammunition. The refueling was interesting to watch because the smaller ships, which were between 50 and 100 feet away proceeding in formation beside the carrier with the fuel hoses stretched between them, would be pitching up and down while the carrier was hardly affected by the waves. For other supplies, a helicopter would deliver them.

The high-performance fighters always burn the most fuel, so we had to fly at maximum endurance power to conserve fuel and limit our maneuvering to 30-degree banks and minimum g loads in order to arrive at the carrier an hour and fifteen minutes later with minimum fuel. Great practice for radar intercepts, in any weather conditions, but pretty boring flying. So our commanding officers of the two fighter squadrons, arranged with the ship's captain to occasionally do what we called yo-yo flights. This allowed the fighters to launch first and recover last with the previous launch, meaning that

CHAPTER EIGHT: Arriving in California and Aircraft...

we had thirty minutes of flight time to take off and do dogfights before having to land.

So we had two fighter squadrons with four jets each to turn and burn without sweating fuel and no tanking. A typical briefing for the eight two-man crews was, "the center of the fight is on the ship's 270-degree radial at 25 nautical miles. Soft deck 10,000 feet, hard deck 5,000 feet, every man for himself." Well, maybe they said a few other things, but that's all I heard! It's called a one v (versus) many scenario. We were constantly looking around for someone trying to get behind us for a shot. Eight F-4 Phantoms trying to shoot each other down was my idea of fun! Flying below the soft deck requires you to stop hard maneuvering and climb. Flying below the hard deck means that you have basically hit the ground and are no longer in the fight. So you operated as if the ocean surface was at 5,000 feet. The soft deck of 10,000 feet would be treated like you were flying at 5,000 feet. Which is actually low when you might be flying at 350 knots pointing straight down! Anyone going below the hard deck would transmit "knock it off," meaning everyone should stop maneuvering. Then the scenario would be set up again, according to the preflight briefing. The other call that would stop the fight was " bingo," meaning that someone had reached the prebriefed minimum fuel state. The person who made the call, having the least amount of fuel in the group, would immediately head back to the ship as the lead aircraft. These same procedures were applied when operating from a land base.

Another flight when we didn't have to worry about fuel was the ACLS calibration flight. It stood for automatic carrier landing system, which allowed the aircraft to land without any pilot input. I landed one time with my hands in my lap because I wanted to see if it really worked! I never heard of any other pilots who tried it. The landing was so good that the LSOs, landing signal officers, standing on a platform next to the landing area, told me not to do any more auto landings. It was for emergency use only. They knew that Chuck Moore didn't manually do it!

Occasionally at night, after flight operations were completed, an aircraft was launched to make one landing pattern to calibrate the system. I got to do it once with a fully fueled Phantom, which meant that I had thousands of pounds of fuel to get rid of to get down to landing weight. So I took the catapult shot with full afterburners, and as soon as I was airborne, I pulled one throttle out of afterburner, left the gear and flaps down, and held full rudder and opposite ailerons to create maximum drag to keep my speed below 200 knots. I also deployed the speed brakes and immediately opened the fuel dump valve. So, with a wide pattern, I got rid of thousands of pounds of fuel and made one landing. My shortest flight ever, less than ten minutes!

The men of Fighter Squadron VF-191, at Miramar Naval Air Station in 1977. The aircraft on the right is the squadron's World War II fighter, the F6F Hellcat. The McDonnell Douglas F-4 Phantom on the left was the fighter that the author flew. The pilot in the middle of the front row is the commanding officer, Denny Moore, an eight-year North Vietnam prisoner of war. The pilot to the right of him is Executive Officer Rod Knudsen, also an eight-year POW. The pilot to the right of him, khaki pants, no cover (cap), is Chuck Moore. The officer on the far left, front row is Tom Holston.

A couple of times, the ship made port calls in Busan, South Korea. The *Coral Sea* anchored in the bay, and the sailors were transported to the city's dock in high-speed ferries. They held about fifty passengers and there were cabin attendants like an airline plane. With

CHAPTER EIGHT: Arriving in California and Aircraft...

thousands of sailors to move, this took several hours. It wasn't a very long ride, but they served refreshments, and it was very nice. After going ashore, we aviators would proceed to the designated hotel and check in for our extended stay. Our squadron had more than thirty officers, so besides our two-man rooms, we had a two-room suite that we called the admin room, where we could meet with others and hang out, pass along information, and keep track of each other. Remember, there were no cell phones. Seeing the city was a great experience, and the people were very friendly and easy to talk to. I love South Korea and its people.

Our flight suits had a pen pocket sewn on the left upper sleeve. I used it to hold my toothbrush and a spoon. You never knew when you might have to divert due to an emergency, and there's zero room for an overnight bag in a tactical jet. Arriving back at the ship after a flight one day, an incident occurred when I broke left to enter downwind and set up for a landing. The standard procedure to land a pair of fighters on land or at sea was to fly parallel to the ship or runway on the right side and in the same direction the ship was going, with the wingman on the starboard, or right side of the lead, at 300 knots and 800 feet. After counting five seconds past the bow of the ship, the lead aircraft would give the kiss-off sign to his wingman and initiate the break maneuver. After an 90-degree bank left roll, you pull max G to slow down, pull the throttles back, and deploy the speed brakes simultaneously. Next, you check your rapidly decreasing airspeed, and at 250 knots, you extend the landing gear and tail hook and deploy the flaps. Rolling level at 200 knots on downwind, you check your gauges. It's a standard procedure, and normally, nothing unexpected happens. But this time, I saw that my hydraulics gauges, there were three, showed two at zero pressure, indicating a major leak in one of my flight control systems. I immediately informed the "air boss," in charge of flight operations on the carrier, of my predicament. He said, "Your signal is Bingo," which meant to turn and head for "the beach," which is what we called the nearest land base.

The only other option was a barrier landing on the ship, when there's no land base within tanker range, where they rig a net across

Helicopters, Jets, and Bush Planes

the flight deck to stop you after touchdown. Your speed without flaps would be way too high for a normal arrested landing. In this case, they sent a tanker aircraft with me so that I could get fuel as needed to make it to the beach. We often flew under a condition called "Blue Water Ops," which meant that we were not in range of any land bases without tanker assistance. So I lost two of three hydraulic systems and had no flaps, no rudder, and a dead wing with no aileron or spoiler. But I had my tail hook! Also, my nose was pointed ten degrees to the left, and I had no brakes. So without flaps, my approach speed was 210 knots, or 242 mph. I planned to touch down just before the approach end arresting gear, on the side of the runway opposite the way I was pointing, knowing that the jet would immediately go to the left side of the runway. All naval air stations have arresting gear cables on each end of the runway for emergency landings of tail hook equipped aircraft. The pilot would plan to engage the cable just after touchdown and stop within a couple of hundred feet. I had Tom grab the ejection handle in case we needed to eject. I only hoped that I wouldn't rip out the arresting gear cable or my hook! But it held, and I came to a stop on the opposite side of the runway. The bottom of my jet was covered with red hydraulic oil. It all went according to plan, no big deal. I even got a good Officer Evaluation Report, with my commanding officer, Denny Moore, whom I calmly spoke to on the radio while en route to Cubi Point writing, "shows no apparent fear of death." Whatever.

During the Vietnam War, it cost a million dollars a day to operate an aircraft carrier. So during peacetime, we tried to operate just enough to keep everyone fully trained and ready for war. That meant half our time was spent at sea practicing our skills and half the time in port, saving money. Even in port, we flew a few missions. Like the time I was tasked with flying the profile of an enemy SAM (surface-to-air missile) attacking a surface ship so that they could practice their missile shootdown procedures. It was a night mission, so I figured I would climb as high as I could and then make a very steep dive toward the ship, like a missile would do. Mostly, I just wanted to see how high I could get just for fun! I was passing 50,000 feet and yelling yeehaw when my backseater got concerned and asked me to stop climbing and get to a

CHAPTER EIGHT: ARRIVING IN CALIFORNIA AND AIRCRAFT...

lower altitude. Above 50,000 feet, if you lose pressurization, as from a bullet or missile shrapnel or anything else, you will die, unless you're wearing a pressure suit, which we weren't. So I reluctantly agreed and tried to make a steep dive toward the ship. Everything was pitch-black and over the ocean. From that altitude, even at idle with speed brakes deployed, I quickly accelerated to Mach speed and overshot the ship by miles! Pretty fun, though.

The F-4 Tactical Manual actually has a procedure for zoom climbing above 100,000 feet. After accelerating to Mach 2 at 60,000 feet, you pull up to vertical. Passing 80,000 feet, the engines will flame out due to a lack of oxygen, meaning they stop running. Hold this position until the aircraft runs out of energy and it begins to fall toward the center of the earth. We referred to this as becoming a lawn dart. Remember to pull the throttles off, and passing 60,000 feet descending, attempt a relight of the engines. I should have tried it.

Because it takes so much fuel, and there being no practical use for flying above the speed of sound, short of catching an enemy fighter, we rarely did it. For one thing, it requires full afterburners. Except on a PMCF, or post maintenance check flight, after major engine work, or overhaul. The checklist requires that you climb above 30,000 feet or go 30 miles out from the coast, over water before exceeding Mach 1 due to the sonic boom it caused. I remember the first time I had the opportunity in the F-4 Phantom. Normally, the pilot and RIO can hear a lot of wind noise, as well as engine noise, even with excellent helmets with hearing protection. After passing through the sound barrier, it is suddenly very quiet and smooth. With the engine air intakes near the front of the plane, there was a faint sound from supersonic air rushing through the fuselage. The normal whine from the big J-79 engines behind you was barely audible as you were outrunning practically all of the noise.

The speed of sound is 761 miles per hour at sea level and varies with temperature, which decreases with altitude at a rate of 3.5f degrees per thousand feet. The F-4 had an instrument that showed your ground speed, and I've seen it approaching a thousand miles per hour with the help of a 200+ mile-per-hour jet stream pushing me eastward. Besides

Helicopters, Jets, and Bush Planes

the quiet, the other major change I noticed was that when I tried to turn, I could roll the wings into a bank angle, but when I pulled the stick back to pull the nose around, I would immediately enter stall buffet, resulting in little turning. At subsonic speeds and low altitudes, the harder you pull, the faster you turn. A stall is produced by exceeding the wing's critical angle of attack. A stalled wing produces little lift. In the thin air, that happened with a very small increase in back pressure, so turning was very slow. Then when I pulled the throttles out of afterburner, my body was suddenly launched forward against my harness due to the instant deceleration from the drag. The SR-71 has a turn radius of more than fifty miles at high speed.

One of my collateral duties as a "nugget," the name for a junior officer on his first cruise, was a position called First Lieutenant. My responsibilities included keeping the ready room clean and orderly, and there were personnel assigned to me for this job. The ready room was where pilots and their RIOs would meet for mission briefings and debriefings, training presentations, and socializing. It was our classroom and our living room. In the evenings, after flight operations were secured, we would watch a movie. That was also my responsibility, so I was always under pressure from my squadron mates to get a good one from the ship's media custodian. Except they were all B-movies and old. Like *Bring Me the Head of Alfredo Garcia* or *Invasion of the Bee Girls*. It had to be an action movie or have scantily clad girls in it. So I would call around to the other squadrons to see what movie they had. If they said something like, "tits in the second reel", I would arrange to swap with them and show two movies. Everything had to be set and tested to ensure that there would be no problems when the switch was flipped on the projector. Also, everyone knew that the commanding officer, who was called Skipper, would be summoned from his nearby room after everyone else was seated, and in complete silence, he would take his special seat in the front. Then at his command of "roll 'em", I would flip the switch turning the projector on, while an assistant would flip the light switch off at the same moment. Then we could be loud again. A lot of pressure! Tradition!

CHAPTER EIGHT: Arriving in California and Aircraft...

Another one of my job titles was Coffee Mess Officer. At a shore base, it called for keeping fresh, hot coffee available throughout the day. On the ship, we had a dining room that was always open, and due to the heat on the un-air-conditioned vessel, most of us would drink a lot, but the ship only served Kool-Aid. So I had a soda mess, where various kinds could be purchased for a dollar. I would order them on shore by the pallet, and they would be delivered to the ship and loaded onto the hangar deck. They only cost me thirty cents each, so I made a good profit. I also had T-shirts made with our squadron name and logo on them, coffee mugs, drinking glasses, Zippo lighters, all kinds of things. Anyway, at the end of the seven-month cruise, I had a lot of money to spend on the squadron end of cruise party, just before the ship headed back to the States. In addition, the carrier air wing arranged a big party for all of the officers from all of the several squadrons, at the Cubi Point Officer's Club.

I arranged to have our own squadron party for the night after the air wing party, just for the Hellcat pilots and backseaters at one of the many bars in the town of Olongapo, outside the base. And it was a little different from the official party at the O'Club on base. In the prior few weeks, I chose the bar and arranged with the mama-san to have a private party. All of the dozens of bars, including hers, had lots of bar girls working there, so that part was covered! I ordered many cases of beer and alcohol, along with roasted pigs and lots of other food. The bars always have lots of loud music and dancing girls on a stage, so what else could we possibly want! This would cost a few thousand dollars, so after paying a deposit, it was all set.

I had met one of the lifeguards at our O'Club pool one day. Her name was Fe, and she was seventeen. In the Philippines, her name is pronounced Fee, but she Americanized it and pronounced it like Faye. When I saw her the week before the big O'Club party, I asked her if she wanted to go to the party with me. She said she did, so we started hanging out together. Fe had nine older siblings, and she lived with her older sister, Nona. Nona was married to Restie, who was an enlisted Filipino man in the Navy. The US Navy allowed Filipino men to serve on their ships, but they were limited to the job of mess cook, meaning they could only work in the galley, the ship's kitchen, and were limited in rank. One day, just before our Hellcats party, when visiting Fe at her sister's house in town, she asked me if I could take her on the ship to see what it was like. I said sure. The *Coral Sea* was tied up at the carrier pier, busily loading all of the fuel and supplies needed for the upcoming two-week crossing of the Pacific Ocean en route to California. While walking down the pier to board the ship, the captain announced over the loudspeakers that everyone had to get aboard immediately and no one would be allowed off because the ship was pulling out in two hours! A typhoon was approaching, and the ship could not be tied up until it passed by, which would take a couple of days. I thought about it and, realizing that the ship would have to pull back in to complete the onloading, I suggested to Fe that we go back to her house. Being a small community, there was no way that a person could claim that they didn't know about the ship pulling out. I learned later that a helicopter pilot and I were the only officers out of hundreds who didn't get aboard!

So for the next two days, we had the restaurants, bars, clubs, and girls to ourselves! The water was so rough that the barge couldn't tie up to the ship, which was anchored in the bay within sight of the town. And the helicopter couldn't fly because of the winds. We were stranded! Darn the luck. All good things come to an end, so after the seas calmed down, and the ship pulled back in, I headed back to the base from Olongapo after saying goodbye to Fe. When I got to the gate, I was arrested by the military police. I was taken to a room where I met with the mama-san, who was owed hundreds of dollars for the party that took place while the ship was anchored in the bay. I had sent word to her with instructions to keep everything that was ordered and have the party without us. I'm sure that she made plenty of money selling all the food and drinks. So, after explaining that her money was in my room on the ship, she agreed to allow the military police to escort me to the ship to retrieve it. When we got there, I was not allowed to go on the ship, so I sent someone to have my roommate bring the cash from my room. That was accomplished, and I was able to go aboard.

Now I was infamous; every officer from the ship's Captain down knew me! As punishment, I had to stay on the ship when we pulled into

Hawaii for two days, as squadron duty officer while all of my buddies went ashore. It was well worth it!

A big event takes place several days before the aircraft carrier arrives at its home port after returning from a deployment. It's called the fly-off, and its purpose is to transfer all of the flyable aircraft off the ship and into the land base. That's way easier, faster, and cheaper than lifting them off with a crane one at a time. Unflyable aircraft would be lifted off the ship after arriving in port. Being one of the single guys, with no family to meet on arrival in California, I was selected to fly one of our Phantoms off the ship. We would not be flying to the ship's home port in San Diego, however. Just after leaving the Philippines, we stopped in Japan and traded all of our newly rebuilt Phantoms with the fighter squadrons stationed there. Their older model F-4 jets were completely worn out.

The name of the carrier there was the USS *MIDWAY*, named for Midway Island, halfway between the US and Asia, where the most important naval battle in history was fought. That's why that carrier was permanently stationed in Japan, as a reminder. If Japan had won, the US would not have been able to defend an invasion on our West Coast! After Pearl Harbor was attacked, we fortunately had two aircraft carriers that were not in port at the time. When they went in pursuit of the Japanese naval forces, they were vastly outnumbered. The enemy had ten aircraft carriers! Four of them were destroyed at Midway.

So my last catapult shot in the Navy would be from the ship to the "boneyard" at Davis-Monthan Air Force Base in Tucson, Arizona, the only American base that makes more money than it spends. The participating pilots would not be aboard when the ship pulled in—a big event. The aircraft would be stored there in the dry desert air or be disassembled and the parts sold to other countries that operated the F-4. There are thousands of aircraft of all types parked there. I didn't know that I would return with my family fifty years later.

Another Navy tradition is called a tiger cruise. The last leg of the voyage from the Western Pacific to the United States is from Hawaii to California. Except for spouses, who have other opportunities to visit the carrier, other family or friends can fly commercially to Hawaii and ride the carrier back to California. Even children over eight years old could go. They get to experience firsthand how the sailors live and work at sea for several days. A bonus is observing flight operations during the fly-off. The tiger cruise is another reason other pilots didn't want to fly off but stay onboard with their guests. I didn't have any family or friends who could afford the trip or that I thought would be interested in my job.

A few years ago, I went back to the boneyard with my wife, Fe and daughter, Kelly. While taking the bus tour through the facility, I saw several different types of jet airplanes parked there that I had flown when I was still in the Navy! I even remembered the tail numbers. I also toured several large hangars with various historical aircraft in them. I saw one hangar that had a WWII B-24 Liberator heavy bomber in it. It had been restored to flying condition and was surrounded by a post and rope barrier so the public wasn't allowed access to the interior or get close enough to touch it. This is the kind that my dad flew thirty-five missions on in Europe in 1944 as a radio operator/gunner. He was in the 467th Bombardment Group. After looking it over, I noticed a map set up beside a long counter. Behind the counter were two older men. One of them noticed me looking at the map and asked what I was looking for. I told him that my dad was stationed at RAF Rackheath in England. He pointed its location out next to the village of Rackheath near Norwich. I said that I didn't know much about his service otherwise. So he asked what his name was. I told him it was Charles Harold Moore, and he started looking in a large book full of names. Then he said, "Here he is. Let me give you some resources to learn about his experience." He handed me a slip of paper.

Weeks later, after I got home, I got on my computer and checked out the websites that were on the note. It turns out that there are several sources of information that include lots of photographs of crews lined up next to their bombers, life on the base, maps of the bases, etc. One website was created by one of Dad's squadron members, so it was particular to his unit. There were copies of bombing missions that had each

CHAPTER EIGHT: ARRIVING IN CALIFORNIA AND AIRCRAFT...

aircraft listed along with the crew's names and the target. Pictures of the nose art chosen by the crews and painted on their bombers inspired us to do the same to our helicopters in Vietnam. One was named *E Pluribus Aluminum*. Another was *Double Trouble*, with a painting of a bottle of whiskey and a scantily clad pin-up. My dad's ship was *Lonely Heart*. I contacted the webmaster and learned that Dad's unit still had annual reunions and that one of my father's crewmates, the last one alive, had recently passed away. I almost had an opportunity to meet someone that he flew into war with. Unlike my war, the crews then were assigned to one airplane, and they trained together in that airplane before flying it across the Atlantic Ocean to England as a unit.

After my younger brother got out of the Army after two tours in Vietnam, he stopped maintaining contact with the family for reasons unknown. I learned later that he had spent time in a Veterans Administration hospital but never knew why. Anyway, a few months before I was scheduled to go on my Navy cruise, I got a call from my grandmother, telling me that he had shown up at her house in West Virginia unexpectedly, was living in Columbus, Ohio, and she gave me his number. I called him and learned that he was an electrician and had a steady girlfriend who had a young son. I asked if I could visit him. A couple of weeks later, my RIO and I flew a Phantom from San Diego to Wright Patterson Air Force Base in Ohio. We had a great visit, and I invited him to come out to California after I was back from my seven-month cruise, which was to start in a few weeks, and we could get an apartment together and plan our futures.

So after the WESTPAC 77 cruise ended seven months later, I called my brother, Paul, and invited him to come and join me. He said that he would get things ready and head on out in a few weeks. My Flight Instructor Pilot Certificate was about to expire. They require renewal every two years, so I signed up for a weekend FAA renewal seminar taking place in San Diego in a couple of weeks. I drove my red Corvette to the Ramada Inn Sunday morning, the second and last day of the course. The course was a series of lectures on various subjects by knowledgeable speakers in the field. After the lunch break, the hundred or more participants settled back in for the final few hours. A tap on the shoulder got my attention, and I proceeded to the back of the room. I was informed that I had a telephone call in the lobby. Through sobs, my little sister informed me that my brother had killed himself while on his way to California. I was in shock. It was unbelievable. I called my mother in Alaska. I don't know what we said, but I told her that I would take care of things.

I was excused from the seminar but received credit for the course. My commanding officer authorized emergency leave for a couple of weeks. According to my brother's girlfriend, he had rented a small enclosed trailer, and after loading his possessions in it, headed for San Diego. Apparently, because of the good memories of growing up in the town of Farmington, New Mexico, he had chosen to end his life there. A train engineer had seen him beside the tracks and reported it. A single-shot 12-gauge shotgun lay beside him. He had placed the muzzle under his chin. His car was parked nearby, but even though I contacted the trailer rental company, the trailer was never found. A note on the dashboard said to contact his mother in Alaska, giving her name and phone number. The local sheriff called her, and she had called my sister since I wasn't home.

I called the sheriff, and he asked me to come and retrieve his car. So I flew there and drove his car back. I sold it to a dealership. I declined an offer to view my brother's body. I had no doubt that it was him and couldn't imagine seeing him that way.

A few months later, in 1978, I was assigned to the Pensacola Naval Air Station in Florida, to VT-10, a training squadron, as an instructor pilot training new naval flight officers. This is where I began my naval career a few years before, training to become a naval aviator. A couple of weeks after reporting for duty, my sister in San Diego called to tell me that my fiancée, Fe had arrived from the Philippines! I had hoped to still be in San Diego when she arrived, but the Navy move came first. Later, I learned that she had practically missed her connection in Hawaii, and they had to hold the plane for her. She was still a teenager and had never been on an airplane before or had to navigate a huge

Chapter Eight: Arriving in California and Aircraft...

airline terminal or clear customs. She could barely speak English! I guess I assumed that she would figure it out. What else could I do? My sister's boyfriend went to the San Diego airport to pick her up, so at least I had that covered! After searching the terminal, he finally found her standing against a wall, crying. Looking for a small Asian teenage girl, George knew it had to be Fe.

A couple of weeks later, she arrived in Pensacola. Americans are spoiled by being allowed to travel abroad without permission from their own country. Many foreign countries don't even require Americans to have a visa to visit there. Not so with other countries like the Philippines. So Fe spent many months traveling to Manila to deal with the bureaucracy to get a fiancée visa, which was granted for the purpose of traveling abroad to marry a foreigner. The US government would forcibly send her back to the Philippines if she didn't get married within ninety days. We tried later to sponsor family members to come but were unable due to the strict requirements.

So at the end of the ninety days, I looked up a justice of the peace in the Yellow Pages and called Bernie C. Woollam. After work on Friday, we drove to his house in my red Corvette, wearing everyday clothes, to get married. His wife was our witness, and I think it cost fifty bucks! (A few years later, when we were stationed near Fe's family members in California, we had another ceremony performed by the base chaplain. I bought Fe a dress, and I wore my formal Navy officer dress blues uniform.) We bought a house in Pensacola in an older neighborhood, that had a small pool. It was great to come home on a hot Florida day and jump in. Next, I brought Fe a car and taught her how to drive. I bought her a brand-new Plymouth Arrow for $3,888! The Philippines only has ten years of schooling, so Fe started working on getting her GED.

We were at Pensacola NAS for two years. It was a great assignment because I wasn't training pilots, meaning I got to do all of the flying. The airplane was the North American T-2 Buckeye, the same aircraft that I learned to fly jets in. You could hardly hurt yourself in it! I could do things that would be dangerous in a swept-wing jet. The squadron was big, with about eighty instructors plus many students.

Two of us had flown fighters. Me and a US Marine Corps pilot. We were assigned to demonstrate various types of spins to the student NFOs. And BFR, basic fighter maneuvers. We would put two flight lessons together and stop in at nearby Keesler AFB for lunch. The students wouldn't eat anything because they were already airsick and had to go do all of that high G turning and burning again. I always ordered two chili cheese dogs with extra toppings. One time, I leveled the aircraft for a few seconds and checked my mirror to see how my student was doing. He hadn't said anything in a while. He appeared to be passed out and wouldn't answer me. So I headed back to base and called for an ambulance to meet me. After parking and raising the canopy, a medic climbed up the ladder and hauled him off. He was fine the next day.

The Marine pilot, John Snakenberg, known as Snake, told me about one of his flights. After demonstrating several aerobatic maneuvers in a sequence, the last one, called an Immelmann Turn, involved holding the aircraft level but inverted. While in this upside-down position, he stopped talking and checked his rearview mirror. He saw that his student had thrown up, and now there was about a quart of barf lying on the top of the plexiglass canopy above the student's head! After several seconds, with no other options, he rolled the aircraft upright, causing the contents of the student's stomach to rain down on him. After getting back to base, he said when the student climbed down, he had a few spaghetti noodles stuck on his flight suit. Another great war story for the bar!

The more adventurous students would ask me to do a tail slide. First, you would point the jet straight up and pull both throttles back to idle, to prevent too much air from going backward through the engine. That would have caused compressor blade stalls, with flames coming out of the intakes. They make loud backfire sounds and can damage the engine. With the power removed, you watch the airspeed unwind, all the way to zero! Then you start sliding backward, but eventually, the tail catches the air, and you go through some crazy gyrations until you're pointed at the ground again like a lawn dart. I say that I'm completely in control while being completely out of control!

CHAPTER EIGHT: Arriving in California and Aircraft...

One day, I was driving my Corvette through the base on my way home after work. It was summer, and I had the T-tops off. A carload of students pulled up beside me, and one of them yelled, "Lieutenant Moore, we're taking Bill to the hospital. He swallowed his wings." I answered. "Cool," as they continued on their way. A tradition called a winging ceremony takes place after a class graduates, and their shiny new US Navy wings of gold are pinned on their uniforms. Afterward, they all head to the officer's club to celebrate. There, the new naval flight officers are lined up, with each man holding a pitcher of beer. With his new wings in it! The idea is to drink the beer and catch the wings in your teeth, then set the empty pitcher on top of your head. The last one to finish gets to buy all of the beer. Occasionally, someone doesn't catch their wings.

So everyone looked forward to arriving at the hangar every day and checking the bulletin board for the latest X-ray showing the position of Bill's wings as they worked their way through his system. The bright gold wings showed up great on the black X-ray. To avoid swallowing one of the little metal buttons that go on the pins to keep the wings on, he had left them off! But like the doctor said, they would go through just fine. He'd seen it before. My F-4 RIO, Tom, told me about his winging ceremony. Tom was of German descent, and naturally, a big beer drinker. He could practically inhale those things. So, wanting to be first to finish, he basically poured the beer down his throat without stopping. At the very end, he said to himself, "Uh-oh," and the entire pitcher of beer came back up and filled his pitcher again. He said he didn't hesitate to chug it back down, and still was the first to finish! Made me proud.

After our maintenance department completed a major inspection on one of our airplanes, I was assigned to perform the PMCF. These flights are done solo, so I took off and headed to the nearest Warning Area. Using a special checklist, I had one last item to complete, involving a climb above 20,000 feet. After that was done, and ready to go to the club for a beer, I pointed the nose straight down, with the throttles at idle and speed brakes out. Man, was I coming down fast, above 300 miles per hour! Passing 10,000 feet, I had just started a hard pull to raise the nose when it felt like someone hit me between the eyes with a sledgehammer! I was also blinded temporarily, and the pain was really bad. I knew that I needed to level off and slow down, and I was already heading for the air station. Gradually, my sight returned, and the pain subsided a little bit. I was relieved, knowing that I was going to make it back. I didn't need to stay in the base hospital, but I got X-rayed every day.

The huge atmospheric pressure change from my steep and fast descent had caused the sinuses above and below my eyes to burst and instantly fill with blood. I must have had a slight cold. The cure was to wait, stay on the ground for a few weeks, and allow my body to break down the huge blood clots and drain from my sinuses. Other than black eyes and a headache for a few days, it was not a big deal. I hated staying on the ground, though.

I was one of the few instructors to get a dual qualification, meaning that I could fly more than one type of aircraft. Very unusual in the military. Besides having dozens of T-2 jets, we had several North American T-39 Sabreliners, originally designed as a business jet. It could be operated by a single pilot and had radar training stations installed in the passenger area to train multiple NFOs in low-level and cross-country flying procedures. An NFO instructor was in charge of the students, who did all the flight planning and preparation, so all I did was fly. Perfect! I also got to choose the cross-country destinations, which included an overnight stay. Usually, I chose to go where my family or friends lived. Due to public scrutiny, we weren't allowed to go to Las Vegas. Rats!

On one of those trips to San Diego, after visiting my sister, I was in base operations, getting ready to head back to Florida when an air traffic controller from upstairs ran down and yelled, "Look out the windows." I looked out and saw a large, black smoke cloud rising from downtown San Diego. It was PSA flight 182. They had just had a midair collision with a small Cessna airplane, which had damaged the airliner's flight controls. All aboard both aircraft, and several people on the ground, perished. The last radio transmission from the cockpit was, "Ma, I love ya."

CHAPTER NINE
Airline Pilot

Military pilots have what we call a payback period after completing flight training. It was four and a half years after graduating and becoming a designated naval aviator. Now, it's eight years. The flight training costs millions of dollars for each pilot, hence the required service commitment. Anyway, most pilots eventually want to get hired by a major airline, with the excellent pay and benefits. Not to mention the safety factor. So the year before your commitment to the Navy ends, you start preparing. First, you need to have the Airline Transport Pilot Certification. You had to pay a civilian flight school for that, but your GI Bill benefits would pay for it. Before the flight training, you needed to pass a special written exam.

One company held weekend prep courses in various cities around the country, just for the many military pilots who were preparing for their future airline jobs. They sent you a book of questions and answers to study. The questions were from the actual test that previous students had remembered. Much of the instruction was on how to apply and use the two dozen formulas that required thorough understanding. Like how to calculate your new weight and balance data after some of your cargo was removed and new cargo added. These formulas had to be memorized. So you were instructed to sit in your car after arriving at the test site and review the formulas before entering the facility. Then, as soon as you sat down, you would write each formula down on sheets of paper before beginning the test. After finishing the test and returning to your car, you would write down any questions and answers that you had not seen before. These would be added to the study guide.

Next, you joined the Airline Pilots Association, ALPA. Then you tried to get applications from as many airlines as you could. It was very difficult to get an application. I recall that the airlines would not just send you one, or give you an appointment to speak with the hiring department. You had to know a pilot who already worked for them to get a recommendation. Then they would send you an application. I remember the chief pilot of the airline that eventually hired me asking me to choose what pilot I would recommend to be called in for an interview from the applicants who had listed me as a pilot who knew them professionally. I tried to recommend all of them, but there were a lot of applicants.

The primary goal was to get a letter from an airline requesting that you contact them to arrange for an interview. It was like an acceptance letter from a major university that you had applied to. Next, you called ALPA and requested they play the tape for the particular airline. This recording would give you some insight into how the interview process for that airline worked, along with some of the questions you would be asked. They were all different. You would be interviewed by several departments, then the chief pilot. The chairman of Eastern Airlines, Frank Borman, previously an astronaut, required prospective pilots to name all the planets in order, from the sun outward!

I got a few interviews before getting a job offer. One was for United Airlines in Denver. They were one of the few airlines that required applicants to take the Stanine test, which was supposed to predict training aptitude. One exercise played a recording of groups of ten numbers simulating being given radio frequency changes. You had a few seconds between to write them down. That was easy for me. I remember a few of the questions. One section tested your memory of cartoon characters. Like who was the neighbor that was always giving a young blond-haired boy advice? Or what was the black duck's name? Other questions might not have a correct answer, but you had to choose one anyway. My favorite was, would you rather hit yourself in the thumb

CHAPTER NINE: Arriving in California and Aircraft...

with a hammer or throw up on a crowded bus? I easily chose hitting my thumb. I later learned that most guys chose to throw up. I apparently passed and was put on the hiring list.

Before United offered me a job, I got a letter from Air Florida Airlines, saying I was hired and assigning me a class date for Miami, Florida. It was a low-cost airline that went bankrupt after my third year there. It was great fun while it lasted because it was a new, fast-growing company, and everyone was excited to work there. The airplanes were mostly all brand-new Boeing 737 airplanes, plus a few DC-10 planes for flights to Europe. Practically all of the flight crews were under thirty-five, and single, especially the flight attendants, whom I will refer to as FAs. We even had a twenty-nine-year-old DC-10 captain. When I was in Miami for my interview, I ran into one of my old Navy flight instructors, Mike Foster. He was doing his Captain upgrade training. I asked him how long he'd been working there, and he said eight months. Unfortunately, the hiring slowed down after I was hired, so I never got enough seniority to bid for a captain position. Later, Mike was killed while flying a WWII bomber for a nonprofit organization.

The way airline pilots are scheduled for flights is a little unique. Every pilot has a seniority number, assigned by date of hire. Pilots hired on the same date went by birth date. Then, any time several pilots applied or bid for the same thing, the lowest seniority number got first choice. There are hundreds of combinations of flying schedules at each crew base due to all of the different routes, times, equipment, days off, etc. The company scheduling department puts these schedules out, which are called flying lines. So every month, every pilot and flight attendant would turn in their bid sheet for their preferred flying lines. The person with seniority number one only needed to bid one line because they would always get their first choice. The person with the seniority number of fifty would need to bid fifty different lines, if they had that many they cared about! When the company announced a new pilot class for thirty new Captains, the thirty First Officers with the highest seniority numbers would get those upgrades if they bid for them. It was the same for flight attendants.

So, after four years in the Army, two years in college, and six years in the Navy, I finally became an airline pilot in 1980 at the age of thirty-three. The first year as a new airline pilot, you are on probation, meaning that you could be fired for any reason. Your job is not permanent, and your pay is poor. The first six months I was paid six hundred dollars a month. It went up to eight hundred dollars a month for the second six months. After the probation period ended, the pay was three thousand dollars a month for a first officer. The captains were paid a lot more. Unable to afford to buy a new house in Miami, I continued to live in Pensacola and commuted to work. Pilots have something called jump seat privileges. This meant that we could ride in the extra seat in the cockpit for free. You just had to sign up for it to reserve it. Lots of pilots chose to commute to live in a city that they preferred. So then, after my year of probation was over, Fe and I could afford a new house in Miami. In 1981, my mortgage rate was over 18 percent! My current mortgage, which I got in 2020, is 2.25 percent. While living in Miami, I obtained my scuba diving certification and my real estate salesman license.

Airline flight crews rarely see the management or go to an office building. The regular workday started with putting on your uniform and driving to the airport, arriving two hours before flight departure. The pilots go to a room above the passenger terminal, with private access, called the crew room, to meet their captain or first officer. The senior flight attendant would also meet with the captain and inform him that everyone else, known as the backend crew, was accounted for. There were usually several other pilots there, and it was great to hang out together for a while. Air Florida had about three hundred pilots, and because of changing schedules and crews monthly, you quickly got to know everyone. Several of our pilots had been in the Navy with me. I even went to college with a couple of them. After a while visiting, it was time to go to operations and get your flight plan and weather report. Finally, we went through the terminal to the gate where our aircraft was parked. The copilot would go down the stairs at the end of the jetway and do a walk around preflight of the plane. Then he would join the captain in the cockpit to begin preparations for the flight. About the

CHAPTER NINE: Airline Pilot

same time, the FAs would arrive and begin preparing the cabin for the flight, checking equipment, galley supplies, etc.

The public only sees the professional side of the crew's interactions, but we always told each other the latest jokes and played tricks on the new crew members. The jokes would often be about airline crew members. And there was always a lot of talk about the company, like what did we think about the latest rumors, of which there were always a few. And of course, everyone had their complaints about rules, pay, scheduling, and other things. So a typical joke would be like, what do you call two pilots in a basement? A whine cellar! Or, what's the difference between a captain and a canoe? A canoe tips occasionally. I know, lame but harmless.

On the back of the center console in the cockpit was a handset that was exactly like the ones on the old black desk telephones. Its purpose was for pilots to communicate with the head flight attendant in the back when flying or to make passenger announcements over the PA system, like the welcome aboard from the captain. There was a ringtone to alert the pilots that the head flight attendant wanted to speak to them, and it had a test button in the cockpit. It sounded exactly like a telephone ringing. If I saw a new FA, especially a young girl just a few years out of high school, in the front of the plane prior to boarding the passengers, I would push the ring test button a couple of times to get her attention. Then I would calmly pick up the handset and say loud enough for her to hear me, "Hello, sure, just a minute." Then I would look at the new FA and say, "Suzie it's your mother." She would look a little surprised but would answer the phone every time! Then we all got a good laugh.

Due to the bidding process every month, you would be paired with a different captain or first officer for the whole month. The flight attendants did the same thing, but their schedules were different from the pilots, so every flight would be with a different cockpit crew and cabin crew. On layovers, we got to socialize a little bit and usually met up at the hotel bar after checking in.

The flying was great, with new airplanes and interesting destinations. I preferred the schedules that had no layovers so I was home every night. That meant more flying days per month but shorter routes. If they weren't between Florida cities, they were to one of the Central American countries. We served the smaller cities, and some had no terminal buildings. One flight path was over an active volcano at a low altitude. Another was over the Great Blue Hole in Belize. There were few navigation systems or radars. Very different from flying in the United States.

During the early 1980s, thousands of Cubans emigrated to the United States, arriving in Florida by private boats. The boats were mostly provided by Cuban residents in Miami. It began with the Mariel Boat Lift in 1980, when the president, Fidel Castro announced that anyone who wanted to leave could go. A lot of them were criminals who were released from prison and put on boats by the government, and many others were poor and uneducated. Eventually, some learned that integrating into American society would be difficult; they could not find work and wanted to go back.

One of our busiest routes was between Miami and New York. The charted flying routes were called tracks, and they were overwater off of the East Coast. On a late-night flight on the tracks from New York to Miami one dark night, while cruising along above 30,000 feet, everything was quiet. Until the ring from the senior FA. She wanted to speak to the captain. It didn't sound good. He quickly hung up the handset and told me that we were being hijacked! And as he pulled the throttles back, he directed me to depressurize the cabin. As we were doing this, he contacted the air traffic controller and declared an emergency while I set the international hijack code of 7500 in our radar transponder. He requested immediate clearance to Jacksonville International Airport as he was turning toward the west. He also requested that the FAA, Federal Aviation Administration, contact the airport manager and have him prepare a plan for our arrival and coordinate with law enforcement.

The captain, Tom Ryon, said that the hijacker had gone to the aft lavatory, pulled out all the paper towels and tissue paper, and piled them around him. Then he opened the door and yelled for a flight

CHAPTER NINE: Airline Pilot

attendant. The senior FA said that while holding a cigarette lighter, he demanded to be flown to Cuba. Now you know why no lighters are allowed onboard. Tom told the senior FA to tell the hijacker that we would take him there, but we had to stop for more fuel first. That was not true, of course. Anyway, we landed at Jacksonville and knew that several law enforcement vehicles were parked in a line on one of the main taxiways near the terminal. After spotting them, we tried to keep the aircraft pointed at them so they wouldn't be visible from the side passenger windows. Everything went according to plan, and no one was hurt. As soon as we stopped with all the law enforcement right in front of us, Tom shut the engines down while I jumped out of my seat, exited the cockpit, and assisted the flight attendant in opening the forward door. Stairs were pushed up to the door, and I ran down first as the law enforcement ran up. Then the senior FA directed the passengers to follow me. I led them to an open grassy area on the opposite side of the aircraft from the terminal.

When the law enforcement officers ran to the back of the plane and grabbed the hijacker, he was so overwhelmed that he didn't even start a fire. Even though a fire/crash truck was standing by, a fire would have been a disaster. Protocol required that all of the baggage be inspected, along with the aircraft, for a possible explosive device. A bomb-sniffing dog was employed to perform the task. It must have been a couple of hours before we could reload the bags and passengers. I let a few of them go to the terminal to use the restroom. When we got everyone aboard, a head count showed that we were a few short. We figured that they decided to take a bus to Miami! What a night.

Dozens of flights were hijacked for a few years, until government intervention stopped it with more security and air marshals. At the same time, Air Florida, as well as other airlines, were providing charter flights to Cuba, and still are, but they aren't free!

Arriving at Miami International Airport from New York on another night flight, we learned that one of the main runways was closed due to gunfire, requiring us to get in line for the other one, on the south side of the airport. I spent a year in Vietnam getting shot at, and now, in my own country! As we entered the landing pattern, we could see several large fires on the north side. Again, during the eighties, Miami experienced several race riots that would last for days.

One winter day, after flying to Texas with another pilot, we had a stop in Tampa before proceeding on to Miami. Normally, everyone was excited and happy with all the new things we were experiencing in our young careers. The captain and I immediately noticed that the gate agent who stepped into our cockpit was not happy and smiling at us. She told us that one of our aircraft had crashed in Washington, and it was national news. On the flight back to Miami, we listened to a commercial radio station and learned how bad it was.

The weather in Washington was especially bad that day, with heavy snow and freezing temperatures. The captain of Air Florida Flight 90 was Larry Wheaton, aged thirty-four. I had flown with Larry several times and from the same airport. On this flight, he had elected not to turn on the engine anti-ice switches when called for by the checklist while taxiing to the runway, saying that he would do it later. There was no good reason to leave the switches off. Then he forgot, an engine probe froze over, and consequently, the perfectly good engines, after setting takeoff power, displayed a higher than actual power output. So setting the correct engine power on the primary gauge actually resulted in only having the engines producing about 70 percent power instead of over 90 percent. After lifting off, the aircraft failed to climb. The copilot said they were descending. The captain said, "I know it." Things happen so fast in the takeoff phase that there's no time to think about what is wrong. Seconds later, after hitting cars on the bridge, the airplane went into the ice-covered river, killing many people. Miraculously, five survived, including flight attendant Kelly Duncan. The copilot was Roger Pettit, a former military fighter jet instructor pilot, the best of the best. The cockpit voice recorder showed that he had questioned the captain's decision to not turn on the anti-ice system when called for. But the captain was always right in those days. Now each checklist item must be completed before continuing the checklist. And if a checklist is stopped for any reason, the pilots must start from the beginning when resumed.

After the accident, all Air Florida pilots were required to experience the same scenario in the simulator. The solution was to confirm

Chapter Nine: Airline Pilot

that the engines were producing full power by comparing two different engine power instruments. If the pilot determines that the actual power output is lower than it should be, and he has already passed the point of being able to abort the takeoff, he should immediately push both throttles to their forward limits, until the aircraft is safely climbing. Prior to this accident, pilots were extremely reluctant to push the throttles to their limit. By design, jet engines cannot be operated at full throttle, except in an emergency. Routine full-throttle operation will damage the engine. But it will operate normally until it has landed to be inspected.

Many airline pilots, most of whom came from a military jet pilot background, elected to join a reserve unit. Not only to earn a little extra money but to continue to enjoy the camaraderie and opportunity to continue to fly complex military aircraft. The life of a military pilot is great, and fun, particularly in peacetime. Actually, wartime flying is great fun, too, even with bullets being fired at you! Especially if you're a single man. We always said, "Big sky little airplane." What are the odds of getting hit? Members of a reserve military unit are required to attend weekend training drills monthly, and two weeks of training annually. In addition, pilots can volunteer to perform additional drills by flying missions.

Usually, the military air base is located in a different city, and even state, than your airline base or where you chose to live. To avoid the several extra days away from home every month, I opted to join a non-flying unit in Miami, where Fe and I lived. It was a small group, and I was the only pilot. There were no aircraft. When it was time to do our annual two-week training camp, our commander arranged for us to go aboard a Navy ship that was going to be at Guantanamo Naval Base in Cuba. We flew there on an Eastern Airlines chartered flight. The ship was the LPH *Iwo Jima*, an amphibious assault vessel operated by the US Navy, and it carried US Marines. It was also the first ship designed and built to be a dedicated helicopter carrier. Perfect, I could fly choppers!

The ship was doing a pre-deployment shakedown cruise, so it didn't have any marines aboard, only the ship's company, which was the Navy crew that operated the ship, and a few naval aviators who would be in charge of the air operations. There were a half dozen officers in our unit, and we met the ship's officers at the O'Club. After introductions, the ship's air wing officers, after spotting my Navy pilot wings, immediately separated me from my comrades. I rarely saw them afterward, except in the evenings at the club. Navy aircraft carriers have an air wing that operates separately from the ship's company. In those days, the ship's company officers wore black shoes, and the air wing officers wore brown shoes. So we referred to each other as a group, as black shoes or brown shoes! The ships have a control tower like airports, which is operated by a senior officer, who is also an experienced aviator. His unofficial title is Air Boss. His assistant, a less experienced junior officer, we called the Mini Boss. To allow the few aviators the ability to stay current, there was one UH-1 Bell helicopter, a Huey, aboard. They soon had me in the pilot's seat, flying around the base and the ship. It had been thirteen years since I'd been anywhere near a helicopter, but like riding a bicycle, I could still fly it! That made my two weeks of annual training really fun.

With a lot of free time, I played tennis every day. The O'Club showed movies on an outdoor screen on the patio. The tropical weather was mild, and I didn't notice any flies or mosquitoes. An ice cream bar was set up, so we could make our own free sundaes, as many as we wanted!

Competition between airlines is always fierce, and our main competitor in Miami was Eastern Airlines. At one point, the cost of a round-trip ticket between Miami and New York was seventy seven dollars! The cost of fuel to fly each seat was more than that. People were going for the weekend. What killed us was the Europe route competition. A businessman named Freddie Laker leased a bunch of Boeing 747 jets to compete with us. So, to get an advantage, the CEO of Air Florida presold thousands of seats on our DC-10 jets at a steep discount. That worked until the dollar crashed, making every flight a big money loser.

When Air Florida declared bankruptcy in 1983, most pilots did the normal thing and applied to other airlines for a job. They would get

CHAPTER NINE: Airline Pilot

hired due to all of the airline experience they gained over the last few years, meaning less training expenses for the new airline. Unfortunately, they started over at the bottom of the seniority list. So a former captain might have to fly copilot, possibly for a new captain with a lot less experience than he had. Some pilots would be furloughed two or three times with different airlines but would eventually get senior enough to be safe from furloughs and retire at sixty.

CHAPTER TEN
BACK IN THE US NAVY

The airline pilot job was great, but I didn't like the uncertainty and change. After I told the chief pilot that I was quitting before getting furloughed, he said that he was giving me a three-year leave of absence instead, allowing me to keep my seniority number in case I might want to come back, in the event that the company survived. So I chose to go back to the Navy, knowing that I could earn a retirement in ten more years. Thus ended my airline pilot career. Another thing we said in the Navy was "I'll take luck over skill any day." I was lucky that I was out of the Navy for only three years; any longer, and the Navy would have hesitated to let me back on active duty. I would have been too far behind my peers on the latest aircraft and technology. I was also lucky that I was in a reserve unit. I applied to go back on active duty, and my unit commander wrote a letter of recommendation, noting my accomplishments and participation in the Naval Reserve. Also, a military officer's commission never expires, so that they can be recalled to active duty if needed. So I was accepted, and due to my recent experience as a jet transport pilot, was ordered to report to a reserve squadron in California to fly the Navy's new McDonnell Douglas C-9B, Skytrain aircraft. That was my third lucky coincidence. Basically, all I had to do was get a haircut!

A few years prior, the Navy saw the need to replace the old propeller-driven transports they were using, so they ordered a new version

CHAPTER TEN: BACK IN THE US NAVY

of the popular airline aircraft, the DC-9. The new C-9 would have a large side cargo door to accommodate various mixes of cargo and passengers. This was made possible by mounting airline seats on cargo pallets. Then you could easily load bare pallets for an all-cargo mission, all palletized seats for a passenger mission, or a combination of half and half. More fuel tanks were added to allow flights from the West Coast to Hawaii, one of the longest overwater routes with no alternates in the world. Also, extra overwater inertial navigation systems would be added that didn't depend on any land-based components. The new airplanes couldn't be built fast enough, so the Navy purchased civilian planes and had them converted and refurbished with new interiors and paint. There were eleven transport squadrons, each with either two or three aircraft, either DC-9s or the military version, the C-9s. The squadrons each had thirty or forty pilots and a couple of hundred enlisted men who performed all of the aircraft maintenance. The airplane was a lot of fun to fly, cruising at .84 Mach, or about 600 mph and up to 37,000 feet. It could go anywhere in the world and was self-contained with its own APU or auxiliary power unit, which was a small jet engine in the tail that was used to start the main engines or run the electrical system and air-conditioning. Tactical military jets like the F4 had to be started with a separate ground power unit, so we always had to be sure that the airport we were going to had a start cart, which meant military bases.

US Navy McDonnell Douglas C-9B flown by the author, over Southern California.

Already having completed ten years of active duty, four in the Army and six in the Navy, I planned to stay in ten more years to attain the required twenty to earn a pension and retire at forty-five. So I did, serving in three different squadrons and flying around the world. The mission was to move naval personnel and cargo. Most flights were within the United States, and like the airlines, would be day flights or overnight trips, staying usually in hotels and dining in restaurants. The crews also received per diem, like the airlines, for time spent away from home. The majority of the pilots and mechanics were reservists, also known as "weekend warriors." Several of the pilots, like me, were full-time active-duty officers who kept the various departments running on a day-to-day basis.

Even though most of the personnel were on a regular eight-hour schedule, the unit operated around the clock, with three shifts. The enlisted men and women could volunteer to be aircrew for a little extra pay but a random work schedule. A normal flight crew would be a minimum of six people. Usually, there was also a trainee with the cabin crew. There were crew chiefs who were responsible for the aircraft's condition and fueling when on a flight, who rode in the cockpit with the pilots and read the checklists. They were experienced mechanics and historically might be called flight mechanics or flight engineers. The cabin crew consisted of a loadmaster, who was responsible for the cargo loading and unloading and computation of the weight and balance on each flight, and flight attendants, responsible for passenger safety and control.

In addition to daily flights around the United States, the Navy also provided intermittent transport services for our various bases around the world. These missions operated as detachments, meaning that the aircraft and crew would report to the area commander and would be under his control for local missions for two weeks or more. Normally, an aircraft and two flight crews would be deployed to the Mediterranean, flying between the bordering countries, and another in the western Pacific, flying between our bases in Asia. The "Med" crews used our

CHAPTER TEN: BACK IN THE US NAVY

base in Sicily as home base, and the "WestPac" crews used our base in the Philippines or Japan.

The standard route to the Mediterranean, starting from the United States East Coast, was to Lajes, Azores, then Rota, Spain, and finally, Sigonella, Sicily. Lajes, a small Portuguese island in the middle of the North Atlantic Ocean, and Rota, the "Gateway to the Mediterranean," were just fuel stops, and Sigonella, in the shadow of Mount Etna, an active volcano, would be our base for the next few weeks.

The standard route to the western Pacific began in California, with a fuel and overnight stop in Hawaii, then Wake Island for fuel and overnight, if the destination was the Philippines. If we were going to Japan, north of the Philippines, then we would go from Hawaii to Midway Island for fuel. Midway is actually an atoll, or ring-shaped island, with a coral rim that encircles a lagoon. Midway Atoll, the most remote place in America, is a national wildlife refuge controlled by the US Fish and Wildlife Service, who I would fly for later. Generally, only government personnel are allowed to visit. I spent a few nights on Midway, where the albatross, or "gooney bird" nests. They got their name from sometimes forgetting to lower their landing gear prior to landing! On arrival at the base, you are soon made aware of the laws pertaining to interacting with the protected species. They build large mounds for nests, and they are everywhere, just a few feet apart. Sleeping with the windows open in my ground floor room, I could hear them making their various sounds all night, just a few feet away. Then, to be allowed to take off to go to Japan, we had to wait until they were clear of the runway.

Usually, during a WestPac deployment, we would arrange for a trip to Hong Kong. The airport arrival procedure is unique and challenging, with a twisting, low-altitude flight path between downtown high-rise buildings towering above you. After arrival, each new pilot was required to attend a briefing by the airport staff, called the CAD (Civil Aviation Department) briefing on the specific operating procedures for Hong Kong Airport. Everyone looked forward to the overnight trip. Hong Kong is a great city for shopping and entertainment. Of course, the pilots had to go to the Bottoms Up Club, famous for the James Bond movie *The Man With the Golden Gun*. Inside were four circular bars set a couple of feet below floor level, each with a topless hostess in the center!

Then there was the shopping trip to Osan Air Base, in South Korea. You have to be very careful when approaching to land to not fly over North Korea. While parking my airplane, I saw a U-2 spy plane taxi by for takeoff, surrounded by multiple government security vehicles. Our flights were open to military personnel stationed in the region, and we often carried staff who were authorized to take a day off from the office work routine. Prices were great, and all sorts of goods were available. The aircrews always purchased a few custom-made flight bags that would have whatever you wanted embroidered on them while you waited. Pilots often took their flight suits to be embroidered with their wings and names. Leather goods, which were expensive in the States, were inexpensive, so baseball gloves and leather flight jackets were popular.

For these three-week detachments, to allow our single aircraft to fly more missions, we would take two complete flight crews. On our day off, we would rent a vehicle and take a trip around the area. The flying was great, the liberty, or time off duty was great, and everyone enjoyed the experience of traveling around the world. Compliments of the United States Navy!

Another fun three-week mission that I had a couple of times was called UNITAS. It is Latin for Unity and is the longest-running multinational maritime exercise in the world. It first took place in 1960 and is conducted annually with the purpose of training forces to conduct joint maritime operations. The most recent exercise featured twenty-six warships, twenty-five aircraft, and seven thousand people from twenty partner nations. It is normally hosted by a South American country and involves operations in both Atlantic and Pacific waters. Our mission was to fly from our base to the naval air station in Norfolk, Virginia, and pick up one of the Navy bands that specializes in pop music. From there, we flew to Roosevelt Roads Naval Station, on the eastern coast of Puerto Rico, to pick up any US Southern Command staff that were involved. Usually, the admiral's wife was a passenger. Next, we proceeded to a South American country, like Peru, for our first of many

CHAPTER TEN: BACK IN THE US NAVY

destinations in Central and South America. From Cuzco, a couple of the crew hiked to Machu Picchu.

Our country, for security reasons, utilizes our military services to promote America and provide a positive experience with our allies—not just the military counterparts but the people who live there. So, while the naval forces of different countries are conducting exercises at sea and in the ports, the Navy band is conducting free concerts at local venues in the cities. American pop music is very popular all over the world, so there were large turnouts for the performances. And of course, the flight crew attended. I was very impressed by how our Navy band members presented themselves. In uniform and professional, they were all exceptional musicians, so they played and sang as well as the original artists. They were very popular, and the people looked forward to seeing them every year.

After a few days in one country, we would fly everyone to the next country as the naval exercises progressed around the coast of South America. One year, after visiting a few countries, we landed in Santiago, Chile. We stayed at a very nice hotel in the heart of this modern and vibrant city. Unfortunately, the people were rioting in protest against the government of General Pinochet. So, after a few days, we were instructed by our superiors back home to proceed to Asunción, Paraguay, and await further instructions as now, our schedule would be changed.

We ended up spending the next week in Asunción in a first-class hotel downtown. We were surprised when Jose Feliciano checked in that same day! He was on a South American tour and would be on the floor above ours for several days. He had about a dozen people with him, including his band, stagehands, and manager. Jose loved the United States Navy, so his crew and mine spent a lot of time together, hanging out at the hotel and going to his concerts. We all rode together in his crew bus. At the concert, as Jose's guests, we were permitted to go backstage or to the areas where the sound engineer or other crew members would be during performances. I usually hung out with Jose's manager, Andy McBride.

One of the most impressive things that Jose did was to start his shows with a perfect rendition of the host country's national anthem.

Helicopters, Jets, and Bush Planes

That always brought the house down, with everyone singing, cheering, screaming, and dancing. Now the stage was set. After performing several of his hits, playing his trademark acoustic guitar, Andy would walk onstage and exchange it for an electric guitar. I had seen Jose perform on television and was mostly familiar with his songs like "Feliz Navidad" and "Light My Fire." I was shocked when he put on his electric guitar and blasted out the Jimi Hendrix song "Purple Haze." I swear he did it better than Jimi! Exciting.

After the show, followed by a few groupies, we all met in our hotel bar. I surprised Jose by presenting him with my United States Navy "wings of gold," which I pinned on his shirt. Then my aircrew did the same with their wings with the band members. They were very impressed. Later, Jose told me that he would like to do a concert for the US Navy, and I told him I would try to arrange for him to be contacted.

In addition to the normal crewmen on this mission, we brought our flight surgeon, a reserve officer who enjoyed traveling with us. He happened to be an ophthalmologist, so he spent quite a bit of time helping Jose with his eyes.

One day I was having lunch at the hotel with Andy, and he asked if I would like to go shopping with him. Their driver picked us up and took us to a large outdoor market. Jose needed a dress for his young daughter's birthday gift. So, after looking at several, we agreed on one, made the purchase, and the mission was accomplished.

Eventually, it was time to go home, so we packed up everyone and headed back to the States. The whole crew was disappointed that we weren't going to Rio de Janeiro, Brazil. For some reason, I made a fuel stop at Trinidad and Tobago, a small dual island nation, near the country of Venezuela. Maybe because I'd never been there! Pretty cool place.

The US Navy uses dozens of trained dolphins to perform various tasks, such as locating and marking things on the seafloor, carrying cameras, patrolling and guarding harbors, etc. They are trained similarly to dogs, but they have sonar, so can locate things underwater over long distances, even when visibility is limited. One mission I particularly enjoyed was transporting them. Several had been captured at sea and

Chapter Ten: Back in the US Navy

were being held in a swimming pool at one of the hotels in Key West, Florida. I took a crew there, and after all of the seats were removed from my aircraft, we just had a big open space with flat metal cargo pallets on the floor.

After a night at a hotel, my crew was invited to help capture the four dolphins. After the water level was lowered, we lined up in the pool with the handlers and corralled them, one by one. When everyone was ready, we placed them in a sling to be safely lifted from the pool. They were then transported to the base and loaded into my aircraft. They were individually carried in canvas slings, attached to metal frames that kept them a few feet off of the floor. Each one had its own handler, who kept them wet by pouring water on towels covering them and speaking to them in a calm voice. We delivered them to Naval Air Station North Island in San Diego. From there, they traveled a short distance to the Navy's Marine Mammal Program in Point Loma to be trained, along with sea lions.

Another interesting Navy exercise is surfacing a submarine through up to five feet of Arctic ice. It was first accomplished in 1959. Submarines routinely operate under ice as it prevents them from being detected by aircraft. They are nuclear-powered, so they have unlimited fuel. But to communicate or launch missiles, they must surface, wherever they are. As my squadron's operations officer, I was contacted by our scheduler, located in New Orleans, and asked if I could get a mission together in the shortest time possible. Of course, I said that I could! I had an aircraft available, so I just needed to put a crew together. Within a couple of hours, we were on our way to the rescue. The mission was to fly to a Navy base on the East Coast, pick up a submarine periscope, and fly it to the West Coast to replace one that was damaged by the ice. The periscope is 60 feet long!

As the squadron pilot standardization officer, I was responsible for all of the pilot training for forty pilots. One of the advanced qualifications allowed the pilot to fly extended overwater routes, which require a totally different approach than overland routes due to the lack of airports for emergency landings, navigation aids, and fuel stops. I would conduct this qualification flight from a coastal base to an island. On the West

Coast, the route was from Anchorage, Alaska, to Adak Island, Alaska, in the Aleutian Islands, a distance of 1,209 miles. The East Coast route was from St. John's, Newfoundland, to Lajes, Portugal, a small island in the Azores with an American base. The flight is a distance of about 1,400 miles. Each of these routes would require two overnight stays. The town of St. John's is a beautiful place surrounded by ocean views and was initially a fishing village. It is the easternmost point in North America and the place where the first transatlantic radio transmission was received, sent from England by Italian, Guglielmo Marconi, in 1901. He invented the idea of globally networked mobile wireless communication! Like the iPad that I'm using right now! There's a monument on a nearby hill where the simple Morse code transmission was received.

After completing our flight to Lajes and back, we enjoyed another night in St John's. It's a very cool city, charming and friendly. The next morning, my crew of seven rode the hotel van to the airport and prepared for our flight home. Everything was going according to plan, until the takeoff. I pushed both throttles forward to the takeoff power setting, checked the gauges, released the brakes, and began accelerating to our calculated liftoff speed of 150 mph. Halfway through the takeoff run, I saw that one engine was losing power, so I immediately aborted the takeoff by pulling the throttles back to idle and deployed the thrust reversers while applying the brakes. We parked the airplane and went back to the hotel for a few more days while our crew chief, who was an experienced jet mechanic, took charge of the maintenance effort. After identifying the problem, a failed fuel control unit, he ordered a new one and joined us at the hotel. Due to our remote location, it took a couple of days to get the new parts. The new fuel control eventually arrived, was installed and tested, and we continued our journey. Occasionally, we got a nice little unplanned vacation!

A similar experience occurred on a qualification flight to Adak, Alaska. After parking the plane, we checked into the only hotel in town and went to dinner. Being a long way from home, we were enjoying our crew rest period. The next morning, after waking up, I looked out of my second-floor window that faced the docks. A fishing boat had just pulled in, and several people were starting their daily activities. I

CHAPTER TEN: Back in the US Navy

quickly dressed and wandered over to watch. I was always interested in the Alaska way of life, and I intended to live there after I retired from the military. A man was loading his De Havilland Beaver floatplane to fly out to his lodge. I talked to him as he worked. He also owned the sporting goods store in the small town and offered guided hunts. He told me that he and his brother had moved there several years ago. Pointing at a large fishing boat tied up nearby, he said that it was his brother's boat and had arrived carrying 77,000 pounds of pollock! Then he pointed toward the end of the bay and said that his girlfriend had killed a nine-foot brown bear there last year. Brown bears are the same as the inland grizzly bear, only bigger, and because of their rich salmon diet they can weigh up to 1,500 pounds.

Later that morning, after breakfast with my crew, the crew chief and I went to inspect the airplane. It had been parked inside a heated hangar due to the winter cold, which causes frost to form on the aircraft. If we had parked outside, that would have to be removed before flight. My crew chief reported that he found a bleed air leak on one of the wings. The hot air from the engine is routed to tiny holes in the leading edge of the wings to keep them ice-free by melting any ice that forms while flying in icing conditions. Being mission-oriented, I checked the en route weather forecast, and seeing no necessity to fly through icing conditions, elected to fly back with the wing anti-ice system disabled. This we did; however, my crew was not happy. They wanted another unplanned vacation!

One way to get a day off was to donate blood at the base hospital. If you scheduled that for the morning, you would have that day off and the next day. We called it vampire leave. You could do it every few months.

I volunteered for every Alaska flight. Besides enjoying the mission, the scenery was amazing. One of the missions was to fly to California to pick up some recent graduates from Navy basic underwater demolition seal training, or BUDS training. The course is so difficult that only a third to half of the candidates complete it. One part of the final training is cold weather warfare in Kodiak, Alaska. The trainees are dropped off on the far side of the island and taught how to survive in the brutal cold with minimal equipment. On the flight up the West Coast, the route to Alaska is over the western border of Canada, and Southeast Alaska. Even above 35,000 feet, on this day, the sky was so clear I could see the ground. At that altitude, you are under radar control and required to fly a specific route and altitude.

Southeast Alaska contains Glacier Bay National Park, a World Heritage Site. It is a popular tourist attraction, first visited by John Muir in the early 1890s. The only access to the park is by boat or airplane. I wanted a closer look, so I contacted the controller and requested a descent to 18,000 feet. Below that altitude, VFR flight is allowed, meaning no more strict rules, so arriving at 18,000, I canceled my IFR clearance. Now I could fly anywhere I wanted, so I descended further to 1,000 feet! Of course, I slowed down from nearly 600 miles per hour to a more leisurely 250 and zigged and zagged my way through the incredible park. In an airliner! Later, I would do the same thing in Glacier National Park, Montana. I'm sure the tourists and pilots in the little sightseeing planes and boats were surprised to see us there.

Occasionally, I had an opportunity for a flight to a naval air station in Maine. We could have boxes of live lobsters delivered to our aircraft. So we took prepaid orders from our comrades and flew them back in the unheated cargo compartment.

In 1992, after ten good years of flying the DC-9 from three different bases to many amazing places, I had enough active duty to retire from the service. So with twenty years of Army and Navy service as a pilot, I put in my paperwork. I was planning on keeping our house as a rental property, so I had a metal building constructed in the backyard, where I could store my possessions. It held all of our furniture and appliances, as well as many boxes of clothes, dishes, cookware . . . everything you have in your house. It also held a Camaro and a Corvette that I didn't need in Alaska. Actually, I would need very little in Alaska since I planned to live in a cabin. I rented our house to a squadron mate, bought an old motor home, and along with my wife Fe, and almost two-year-old daughter Kelly, headed to Alaska. I retired as a lieutenant commander and was forty-five years old. That was the last full-time job I ever had! Another adventure was about to begin.

PART THREE

ALASKA 1993–2025
AGES FORTY-SIX TO SEVENTY-EIGHT

CHAPTER ELEVEN
Alaska Bush Pilot

While I was in the Navy, whenever I was reassigned to a new base, I would buy another house and rent out the previous one. I always chose an average-size house with three bedrooms, two bathrooms, and a two-car garage. Not a new house or an expensive one but a good one in a nice neighborhood, where a regular family could afford to live. So, in addition to my military pension, we had some rental income from three houses. I also purchased a duplex in Alaska, which I rented out. I noticed that the rent was below market, so after the purchase, I raised it. The rental income from one unit now covered the mortgage payment for both! One of the houses was in Miami, Florida. Three months before I retired from my base in Washington state in 1992, category five Hurricane Andrew, the strongest and most damaging storm to hit southern Florida ever, destroyed my neighborhood. It blew the roof off of my house. I watched the hurricane's path on the news, but I had no way to contact anyone there. Power lines, phone lines, and trees were down everywhere. A couple of days later, my insurance company called and told me that the neighborhood was inaccessible, the house was unlivable, and they were sending me three months' rent. I had no way to contact my renters. I never got a letter or anything, so I'll never know what they experienced. When I left the base three months later, we went to Alaska via Florida. After visiting family in California along the way, we arrived at our property, where the

CHAPTER ELEVEN: Alaska Bush Pilot

roads had been recently cleared of debris. There was still no electricity or other services available. Many houses were destroyed by the tornadoes contained in the hurricane.

We parked our RV in the driveway, had a dumpster delivered, and hired a crew for the cleanup. After the roof came off, the wind and rain ruined everything inside. The standard construction method in the area was to build on a concrete slab foundation. To prepare for rebuilding, everything was removed except the slab, wooden stud walls, and electrical and plumbing. The sheetrock walls had solid mold halfway to the ceiling. All of the furnishings were tossed around and ruined. When we first walked in, surveying the destruction, we made our way to the master bedroom. The closet was still full of clothes. I opened a drawer and found a baby's hospital bracelet and a lock of hair among all of the items there. It appeared that the renters had quickly grabbed a few things, got in their vehicle, and left. Probably scared for their lives. Then they had to get on the roads with tens of thousands of others trying to escape north!

With so many homes destroyed, the previous occupants had crowded in with family or found other temporary housing. The lack of housing made my property more valuable as it was in a desirable neighborhood and ready for rebuilding. My insurance company had automatically paid me the market value of my home but didn't want the lot, so that was still mine to sell. The telephone lines were down, and cell phones were not common. After the house and property were cleaned up, I ran an advertisement in the newspaper for my lot, saying I would sell to the highest bidder on a particular day. I took the best cash offer and ended up with a nice profit. Now we could head to Alaska, 5,000 miles to the northwest.

My mother had purchased a small weekend cabin in the town of Willow, Alaska. It is a very popular place for the people living and working in Anchorage to go on weekends because of the access to the Susitna River that runs through the large valley between Anchorage and Fairbanks. Due to the shifting glacial silt riverbed, and the tons of ice during spring breakup, there are no bridges to

Helicopters, Jets, and Bush Planes

access the west side. Hence, there are no roads for hundreds of miles to the west coast. Rivers in Alaska are our highways through the wilderness, which we call the bush. Most native villages are located on rivers, allowing travel by boat or snowmobile. In winter, they use a road grader to make an ice road between the largest villages, and they have a van taxi service.

While I was still on active duty in the Navy, and a few years away from retirement, I took a week of military leave to visit my mother. We stayed in her cabin in Willow. I flew commercially since it would take almost a week to drive there. I noticed that there were no subdivisions in Willow or anything else that a typical small town in the lower forty-eight would have. There was a gas station, a log church, a small post office, an elementary school, and a few other things. Anything else was 30 miles away. Some people lived in regular houses, while others in small cabins. There are no building codes in Willow. Many people living and working in Anchorage would buy an unimproved lot, usually accessible from a dirt road, and spend their summers working on it. These were weekend recreational cabins. They first cleared the trees, which were saved for firewood, then used equipment to make a driveway and pad for a cabin.

If a person had enough money, they would buy a lot on a lakefront or with a mountain view. If they had a riverboat and were adventurous, they would get a remote piece of land on a river. They would access it in winter with snowmobiles. The lucky ones had an airplane. In Alaska, we change the landing gear according to the season. Floats, skis, or wheels with up to 35-inch tires! If there are no runways where we want to go, we land on gravel bars in the rivers or a relatively flat area in a mountain valley. The Piper Super Cub only needs a few hundred feet to land or take off. Also, in Alaska, it's legal for airplanes to use the highways and roads, as long as they don't interfere with normal vehicle traffic.

Owning a small airplane, I was looking for a lot on an airstrip. My mother took me to a facility that was being built near Willow that was next to the river and had a dirt airstrip. Perfect! I chose a lot on the strip and bought it the year before I retired. The facility was owned by an "S" corporation, with about a dozen members, and

CHAPTER ELEVEN: Alaska Bush Pilot

I bought shares in that, which gave me unlimited use of the facility, primarily the boat launch, saving the cost of parking and launching fees. I still have my shares.

So the next year, I took two weeks of leave and drove my Jeep to Alaska, taking my wife and our year-old infant daughter. We tent camped from Whidbey Island, Washington, through Canada to Willow, Alaska, about a weeklong trip. I remember waking up to snow one morning! This was the year before I retired. I planned to leave my Jeep there and fly back to Washington.

Back to the RV trip after retiring. So with business taken care of in Florida, we were finally on the road north! Traveling by motor home is my favorite way to travel. There's no schedule. Up until now, my entire adult life had been strictly regimented, radically different from most people's. With an RV you don't need hotels, restaurants, or reservations for anything. We don't like RV parks, with dozens of others all around you. If you can't find a free and private spot anywhere, there's always Walmart camping! In Canada and Alaska, there are lots of places to park overnight beside the highway. Usually by yourself and free! Just use one of the numerous pullouts or take the little side road down to the creek.

The road trip is incredible, even after two dozen times. The scenery, the wildlife, the huge lakes without a single cabin, the remoteness, and millions of square miles of mostly pristine wilderness. Particularly near sunrise and sunset, you are likely to see game animals. The wary ones hide and sleep in the daytime and feed at night. Most people travel to Alaska in the summer, and on June 21st, the solstice, there's not much night! Moose are the most common big game animal, so you'll likely see those. If you're lucky, you'll see a bear or caribou. Dall sheep on the mountain sides are common, too.

After about a week, we arrived in Willow and parked our old RV on our lot. Home! It was April 1, 1993. Retired and forty-five years old! The four feet of ice melts off of the nearby river the first week of May, and the salmon arrive a couple of weeks after. So I needed a good fishing boat because the glacial water is always ice cold and running along up to ten miles per hour. Extremely dangerous, and many people have died from getting thrown out of their boat or going through the ice on their snowmobile. The salmon, after spending from five to seven years in the ocean, head back to the stream where they were born to spawn and die. They come in waves by the thousands for a few short summer months.

You need to travel on the major river to reach the smaller rivers that branch off into smaller and shallower creeks and streams. That's where you catch them with medium-weight spinning gear, baited with a lure or salmon eggs. They travel through the major rivers between the ocean and the creeks, but they don't take bait, and the water flows way too fast for fishing. Because the glacier water has so much silt in it, it is opaque, so you can't see the bottom. And there are sandbars everywhere, maybe inches below the surface. Even using jet boats and airboats, every boater will get stuck occasionally, especially when they are first learning to run the rivers. I bought a used boat, commonly called a jet sled, due to the mostly flat bottom and outboard engine with a jet unit instead of a propeller, which would run in less than a foot of water without hitting bottom. With my friends and family, I've caught hundreds of salmon and enjoyed running the rivers for years.

Now with our old motor home parked on my airstrip lot, along with my Jeep and jet boat, all that was missing was my airplane! I had left it at the airport near our Washington home, where I retired from the Navy. The summer ended too quickly, after catching and preserving more than a hundred salmon. That first winter, we parked the RV behind the main building at the entrance to the facility. It was not suitable to spend the winter in. On the first floor of the building was a counter where anyone wanting to enter the premises could check-in and pay the fee for vehicle parking and boat or snowmobile launching. Upstairs was a bedroom and bathroom. The building was powered by a generator in a separate shed. As a shareholder, I was offered the job of caretaker for the winter, which allowed us to meet everyone who had a cabin upriver. Several of them lived there year-round, traveling the two or three hours to the road system by boat or snowmobile.

CHAPTER ELEVEN: Alaska Bush Pilot

Finally, spring arrived, and our goal was to get a log cabin constructed on our lot. So we had a 16-by-20-foot log cabin with a loft built. We were the first residents in the area, and of course, there are no services like city power, water, or sewer available within miles. All of the homes in Willow have their own wells and septic systems. There are power lines along the highway but none where our cabin was. If you want electricity, you have to run a generator. Remote villages, mining camps, and hunting lodges all run large diesel generators around the clock. We didn't need constant electricity, used an outhouse like all remote cabins, and carried water from town in five-gallon containers.

The author's wife, Fe, and daughter, Kelly, in front of their log cabin home near the Susitna River in Alaska, in the late nineties.

There were radio telephones and early-model cell phones, but they didn't work where we were. Heat was provided by a wood-burning stove. Air-conditioning was not necessary in Alaska, as it rarely reaches 80 degrees outside. The cabin was built with three-sided milled logs, so the interior walls were fairly flat. I kept a small pile of nails and a hammer on one windowsill. If I wanted to hang something up, I'd just bang a nail in the wall. I got a small propane refrigerator out of an old pickup camper and bored a hole in the log wall for a line from a five-gallon bottle of propane outside. That also provided fuel for a two-burner propane camp stove for cooking. Sometimes, in winter, when the temperature drops to 40 degrees below zero, the regulator on the propane bottle would freeze up and not allow gas to go through. The solution was to pour a pot of hot water or hot coffee on it. No problem!

For lights, a lot of cabin owners install propane lights, connected by copper lines. Keeping things simple, we used hurricane lamps with kerosene in them. Whale oil would have been better with no odor or smoke. I used two for reading books in the winter. No TV! Very little time is spent indoors in summer, so winter is the time to hibernate. Baths were taken in a washtub set in front of the wood stove. My wife, Fe, liked winter because we always had hot water from melted snow in a large pan sitting on the stove. In summer, we used a solar shower, basically a plastic bag with a small gravity spray nozzle, hung on a nail outside. We filled it with warm water from a teakettle. It worked just fine.

Our daughter, Kelly, was two years old that first summer, so no worries about school for a while. We spent most days fishing and boating. With no freezer, like everyone else in cabins, we canned our fish in tin cans or jars. You could even do it creekside. All you needed was a camp stove, pressure cooker, tin cans or jars, and a mechanical can sealer. We smoked a few, but that's a snack, not a meal. Years later, when we had a freezer, we either froze them whole or filleted and vacuum-sealed them.

As winter approached, I bought a used snowmobile that had a long seat on it. Alaskans call them snow machines. We could all fit on it—Fe behind me and Kelly in front. I would put a cargo strap around Kelly and me so she could sleep on the trail. We often went upriver to visit friends who lived there. The ride takes a few hours, so occasionally, we would spend the night.

One Christmas, we rode upriver to spend the holiday with friends. They always warn guests to watch their heads when entering the low

CHAPTER ELEVEN: ALASKA BUSH PILOT

doorway of their tiny log trapper cabin. We cut and decorated a small spruce tree that was nearby, and after dinner, slept on the floor. After the celebration and breakfast the next morning, it was time to go home. The temperature was 35 below zero. After a couple of hours on the trail, we were back at our cabin. It was 35 below inside, too, of course, so before taking our heavy coats and boots off, I started a fire in the wood stove. Kelly had acquired a goldfish, and when we left, I had no way of knowing how cold it would be. Besides, there were no neighbors to leave him with. The little fishbowl was solid ice. I moved it before she noticed it. And I learned that goldfish do not thaw out and start swimming around again! Another thing I learned was that frozen canned goods can be used, but they are very mushy and not very appetizing. We ate them anyway.

After that, I bought a propane wall-mounted heater that did not require electricity, just to keep things from freezing in our absence. It wasn't a good primary heat source as propane is expensive. But it was great to come back to a cabin that was above freezing inside. The least expensive heat is with wood, especially if you can harvest, cut, and split it yourself. Next is heating oil, which is the normal method of heating homes here today. Natural gas is the cheapest heating fuel after wood, but it's not available in Willow. Power outages are common in Willow in the winter, sometimes for hours. So a backup heat source, if you have electricity, is always recommended. For the cabin I used the snow machine to harvest firewood from the nearby woods, using a chainsaw and pulling a sled.

The next spring, a buddy and I flew commercially to Oak Harbor, Washington, where I had retired from, to get my little two-seat airplane and fly it to Alaska. By this time, I had become a little bushy. Meaning I had a full beard and a long ponytail. I always told my Navy pals that when I retired, I would throw away my watch and my razor. And I did! I also wore suspenders and a campaign hat. My friend wanted to see where I worked as a Navy pilot. My squadron was in a large hangar at Whidbey Island Naval Air Station, and about a hundred sailors worked there. I was very familiar with the place, and the people, as I'd been there for four years as a senior officer. So I was walking around like I owned the place, and I could see people looking at me, wondering who

Helicopters, Jets, and Bush Planes

I was. They didn't recognize me at all! They only knew me as a very well-groomed professional naval officer in uniform. Eventually, they figured it out, and everyone wanted to talk to me. I noticed that the new people would ask someone who I was. I took my friend out to the flight line and climbed aboard one of our DC-9 passenger jets, giving him a tour and taking pictures sitting in the cockpit. He was pretty impressed with the whole operation.

The flight to Alaska was very different from a flight in the lower forty-eight. Canada is similar to Alaska in that there are few roads or towns as you proceed north. We followed the longest runway in the world, the Alaska Highway! If you don't, you are taking a huge risk in the event of an emergency. Many pilots have never been found. You will fly over thousands of acres of wilderness, with the few facilities available spaced out many miles apart along the highway. Also, all of the airports are located in the few towns along the highway. After parking the plane, my friend and I would catch a ride to a hotel or lodge with anyone heading that way. Same thing the next morning. There were no taxis in the little towns, so someone would always offer a ride.

Toad River, in northern British Columbia, is a highway service community located in the mountains of the northern Rockies. The gravel runway is beside the Alaska Highway. The facilities are on the opposite side, so to refuel my little airplane with car gas, I taxied across and pulled up to the pumps between the cars and pickups. As I proceeded to fill my tanks, tourists in the restaurant came out and took pictures. My plane didn't have an electrical system, so I had to hand prop the engine to start it. And of course, I looked like a real bush pilot!

Now my Alaska life was complete—cabin, Jeep, jet boat, snow machine, and an airplane in my yard. I also acquired the ubiquitous Honda three-wheeler, the predecessor to the four-wheeler. Summer days were long and sunny, allowing lots of time for outdoor activities like fishing and flying. Conversely, winters were long, dark and cold! Younger people loved the winter because, with a snowmobile or ski plane, you could go to places that were inaccessible in summer. With several feet of snow covering all the brush and dead trees on the ground, and a few

CHAPTER ELEVEN: Alaska Bush Pilot

feet of ice covering the raging rivers, lakes, and streams, you could ride a snowmobile from your house to the western coast. The biggest winter races cover over a thousand miles of wilderness by dog team, or more than 2,000 miles by snowmobile. And the winners do this in less than ten days by dog team and sixty hours or so by snowmobile, mostly in the dark, and often reaching a hundred miles per hour!

The major rivers are busy year-round, with everyone at their weekend cabins, especially during the holidays. Hundreds of snowmobiles and lots of airplanes running around visiting and playing. Where there were lodges or several cabins, a snowmobile would pack the snow down, pulling a homemade drag, to make a runway for ski planes. Sometimes, I would fly out to visit friends, or have a hundred-dollar hamburger at a lodge! Winter flying is a lot of work, especially if you don't have a heated hangar, and park your airplane outside. The snow has to be swept off of the wings and tail feathers because it can get heavy enough to damage your aircraft. During a particularly heavy snowstorm, you might have to get up and drive to the airport to sweep the snow off of your airplane in the middle of the night. To keep ice from forming on the flying surfaces, we kept wing, windshield, and tail covers on them while parked. The engine was wrapped in a heavy insulated cover to keep the heat in when you shut it down for a while or you wanted to heat it up to go somewhere.

But again, in winter, you could land in lots of places. In summer, you would need a dirt strip or a gravel bar on a river. Long, flat areas are hard to find close to where you need to go, like for hunting and fishing. A lot of guys prefer floats on their planes because of all of the water available to land on in the summer.

In 1994, after my first year of retirement, I decided that we could afford to build a new house for Fe's family in the Philippines. Fe took three-year-old Kelly, and I stayed in Alaska while the work was being done. The one that she was raised in, and where we stayed when I went to meet her family was very small and rustic, with no indoor plumbing or electricity, thin wooden walls with no glass in the window openings, and a thatched roof. She replaced it with a large cement house with plumbing and electricity, glass windows, and a metal roof. After Fe and Kelly had been gone for six months, I went to see the progress. I also missed them a lot. Kelly didn't remember me and didn't speak to me for a few days. It took the two dozen workers another two months to finish the project, but it was a great improvement. I remember the skilled workers, like carpenters, were paid four dollars a day and the regular laborers two dollars. There was electricity, but no one had any power tools, so the house was built using only hand tools, most of which were handmade. None of the workers had motorized vehicles and rode bicycles to work, if they had one. Most of them walked. The contractor had a small motorbike. Cars and trucks were rare, except in the large cities. Even there, most people traveled by Jeepney, old American WWII jeeps that were lengthened to carry passengers, which cost a few cents.

The two-mile-long narrow dirt road to the barrio was mostly used by people walking to the bus stop on the highway. Fe had two above ground cisterns built to collect rainwater from the house roof, which was used for cleaning, laundry, cooking, and cleaning the pig stalls. With no stores in the rural area, people raised pigs and chickens. There was no beef because all of the cleared areas were used to grow rice. The property had several coconut trees, papayas, bananas, jackfruit, and other fruits. No apples, oranges, peaches, or grapes like Americans think of, but fruits common in Asia. The doors and some of the furniture for the house were made with Philippine mahogany, a beautiful wood, from trees that were planted many years earlier by Fe's aunt.

Our house in the Philippines is still home to about ten family members, mostly nieces, nephews, and their spouses and children. Fe and I visit every year or two for a month or so.

After a fun four years in our cabin, Kelly was old enough to go to school. No one lived around us, so with no bus service, I had to drive her several miles to the Willow Elementary School, our only school. My old Jeep never got very warm inside, so we had to wear our heavy winter gear. Since there was no electricity to plug an engine heater into, I had to go out in the dark and cold about an hour before leaving to heat up the engine so that it would start at 20 or 30 degrees below zero or

CHAPTER ELEVEN: ALASKA BUSH PILOT

colder! I had a three-foot section of metal stovepipe with a 90-degree elbow on it. I would place that under the Jeep, with the elbow pointed at the oil pan. I also put an old sleeping bag over the hood. Then I would light my weed burner attached to a bottle of propane and stick it in the open end of the stovepipe for forty-five minutes. Easy!

Homeschooling is very popular in Alaska. Not only because a lot of people don't live in a town but also because they want more control over what their children are learning. I also thought there was a lot of wasted time, with assembly, recess, fire drills, nap time, or teacher days. Not to mention the curriculum. So for Kelly's fourth grade year, I decided to become a teacher. I would run it a little more like the Army! Not really. I was actually thinking about staying in our little warm cabin and not having to heat up the Jeep. I was going to concentrate on the three Rs, reading, writing, and arithmetic, like the early schools. So I chose Calvert Homeschooling and purchased the curriculum called, a box of books. The box contained several books of various sizes, all with the same yellow paper cover and no artwork. The three Rs were the most comprehensive books, complemented by other books covering history, science, and geography. What's geography? We have had mail come to Alaska via Arkansas, and when giving our two-letter code to someone on the phone, they frequently get the AK vs AR confused. Then I say, "Oh you must have skipped the fifth grade!"

We kept a strict schedule, with few breaks, studying every day, except for the major holidays, and completed the course early. It was fun, but too much like a job for me. So the next year, Kelly went back to school with her friends. Her teacher saw that she was far ahead of her classmates, so she skipped a grade. The next year, for seventh grade, she had to ride the bus for an hour to get to the junior/senior high school. She came home and told me that she had to carry all of her books all day because her locker combination didn't work. So after several days with no one helping her, I went to the school to complain. A new school was being built, but with six grades in one school, the youngest students, like Kelly, were being run over by the senior high football players. So I decided to come out of retirement and teach one more year. It was a little more laid-back this time!

Helicopters, Jets, and Bush Planes

One morning in 1996, back when Kelly was in first grade, and I was driving her to school, one of the other parents noticed my hat with the airplane on it. She asked if I was a pilot, and I said yes, and I have an airplane. Her husband had a hangar at the local airport, where he did aircraft maintenance, was always ready to meet new pilots, and the coffee was always hot. So I started stopping by Eddie's hangar every morning for coffee after dropping Kelly off. The school and the airport were about a quarter mile apart. Willow Airport was located beside the highway between Anchorage and Fairbanks. It was built as an emergency runway for the female pilots who were delivering American military airplanes to the Russians, our allies during WWII. The exchange took place in Fairbanks. I've seen photographs of the American and Russian pilots dancing at the Officer's Club.

The Willow Airport has no commercial aviation service, other than a couple of air taxi operators with small airplanes, and no paved runway or taxiways. There are several aircraft maintenance hangars and a few personal hangars, but most airplane owners park them outside. In the winter, they pay someone to sweep the snow off or do it themselves. Unlike the airstrip next to my cabin, the state of Alaska plows the runway and taxiways, allowing the use of wheels year round. So before I could afford skis, I started parking my airplane there in the winter.

Also at Eddie's hangar was CPA Air Service, a one-man operation with one bush plane, an M-7 Maule, a four-place tailwheel airplane with a powerful 230 horsepower engine and large, soft tundra tires, enabling landings on short, rough bush airstrips. It also had skis for winter flying. My little two-seater had only 85 horsepower, so was limited to longer strips, which aren't very common in the bush. Regular graded dirt runways are only found in remote villages or at scattered lodges. I could land on the longer gravel bars in the rivers or on a long, flat beach, but the Maule was much more versatile. The owner asked if I would be interested in flying it for him because, during busy times like hunting season, he couldn't do it all himself. I really liked having my freedom, with no commitments or responsibilities or stress! But after thinking about it for a few days, I agreed to help out. There were just too many

CHAPTER ELEVEN: ALASKA BUSH PILOT

pros, compared to the couple of cons. First was that Tom was one of the nicest people I've ever known. He was a military veteran, like me and Eddie. I had been an Army gunship pilot in Vietnam, and Tom had been an Army infantry officer in Vietnam.

The Maule was as fun to fly as I thought it would be. Plenty of power and enough cargo space to carry most of a moose after removing the rear seats. All Alaska hunters hunt moose. They are not too difficult to find and are regularly seen around the cities and towns. Of course, you can't hunt there. But the ones that are legal to harvest are the largest bulls and the youngest bulls, leaving the cows to produce calves. Since the biggest bulls fight each other during the rutting season to gather as many cows together as possible, many can be killed by hunters as not many are needed. The revenue from hunting licenses is used to manage the population and control predators. But besides the enjoyment of the hunting experience, moose meat is excellent, and there's lots of it! A large bull will have hundreds of pounds of meat, which can be processed into a year's supply of steaks, roasts, and burgers.

The biggest challenge is getting into moose country. The few roads, with fewer pullouts, are quickly crowded with pickup trucks and hunters with four-wheelers. Some guys build a moose buggy, basically a four-wheel drive truck with tall tires and no body. Just a chassis with an engine, running gear, a couple of seats, and a steering wheel. They can drive these several miles up a riverbed because, in the fall the glaciers aren't melting and the water upstream is shallow. The next easiest way to get out to the hunting areas is by jet boat or airboat where there's enough water. Unless you're fortunate enough to own one or have a good hunting buddy who does, you'll find that you can't rent or hire one.

By far the best way to get into the country is by aircraft. The guys who can afford to learn to fly, and then buy an expensive airplane, have the most opportunity to have a successful hunt. Their choice of aircraft is always the Piper Super Cub due to its ability to get on and off of a 200-300 foot relatively flat, rough piece of tundra or gravel. A drawback is that they don't have a lot of cargo space, so hunters need

Helicopters, Jets, and Bush Planes

to make many trips to get their moose out. But the Cub's performance is impressive. It is also the first choice for wolf hunting, where you shoot them from the air through the open side door. When there are too many wolves and they are killing too many moose, the state pays a bounty for them. Many hunters, especially if they aren't Alaska residents, hire air taxis to take them out into the country. That's called a drop-off hunt. The pilot will pick you up at the prearranged time, weather permitting. You can also arrange for an expensive guided hunt, which includes outfitting and flying.

I would have loved to have a Super Cub, but due to their popularity, they were very expensive for me. So I sold my Cessna and bought a 1957 Piper Tri-pacer, converted to a tailwheel configuration, commonly called a Pacer.

So wouldn't helicopters be better for hunting? Of course, but the game wouldn't stand a chance of survival. Therefore, helicopters are outlawed from having any part in hunting, such as spotting, hauling game, or establishing and supplying a camp. Even hunters flying in by commercial airplane are prohibited from hunting on the same day as flying and must wait until the next day.

Hunting season is in the fall for most game. There's also a spring bear hunt, when the bears come out of their dens after hibernating all winter. With the Maule, I flew drop-offs, primarily in the western Susitna River valley, on the eastern side of the Alaska Range. The country was beautiful, and flying there never got old. Some of the crude airstrips were more challenging than others, but they all required your full attention. The many airplane wrecks every year is the reason why a lot of pilots can't afford insurance. The businesses that can get insurance pay dearly for it. Big game in the area included moose, caribou, bears, and sheep. Alaska Dall sheep are all white, and the rams stay in the most difficult terrain, but the meat is even better than moose. Only the toughest hunters go after the sheep. A good friend of mine, Phil Stanger, says that you get addicted to it. Where he hunts requires crossing a couple of raging glacial rivers and the use of technical climbing skills and ropes. Then you might spend several days on the mountaintop, unable to see in heavy fog.

CHAPTER ELEVEN: Alaska Bush Pilot

Flying hunters into the area where they would set up their camp, then hunt for the next several days, was a lot of fun. On the scheduled day, I would return to pick them up and haul any meat they had on a separate trip. Hunting regulations require that hunters pack out all the meat before the antlers, to discourage hunting only for trophies and leaving meat in the field. Since shipping hundreds of pounds of meat from Alaska to a lower forty-eight state is expensive, some out-of-state hunters donate the meat to the nearest village. Food Bank of Alaska welcomes wild game meat and fish donations, which they process into one-pound ground meat packages, free for families in need. The antlers on a large bull moose are huge, sometimes spanning five feet or more, and if I couldn't fit them inside my airplane, they would have to be sawed in half and reattached later. Some pilots have carried them on a floatplane float or tied to a wing strut. They're pretty heavy, so something of equal weight would be tied to the other wing. In winter, Cub pilots frequently have snowshoes tied on a wing.

After hunting season was over, I had a different kind of flying to do. Alaska has more than two hundred native villages located in remote regions, commonly only accessible by air or water. The state has built dirt airstrips at the villages for mail delivery and emergency medical evacuation. Since Alaska is one-fifth the size of the lower forty-eight states, most villages are hundreds of miles from Anchorage or Fairbanks, where a hospital is located. Because of the low demand for flights and lower profits, tickets are very expensive, so the villagers don't travel much. The population ranges from a few dozen inhabitants with no stores, to several hundred residents and regular businesses. Travel between nearby villages is by small outboard-driven boats in the summer and snowmobiles in the winter. Even in the smallest villages, there is a school, a clinic, and sometimes, a small store, rarely with any fresh bread, meat, or produce. Canned meats even include bacon. It is very salty, so it must be rinsed before cooking.

The owner of CPA Air Service, Tom Baird, would drive to Anchorage and fill his van with fresh goods purchased from Costco. The next day, weather permitting, we would load up the groceries in the

Maule, and I would fly to a village to sell them. The primary villages were Lime Village and Stony River in the south and Nikolai and Takotna in the north. They were located in the central part of Alaska, on the western side of the Alaska Range, along the Kuskokwim River. I would alternate between the two pairs every few weeks throughout the winter. The Alaska Range contains Denali, also known as Mount McKinley, which is 20,320 feet tall, but the highest mountains that I had to fly across were about 10,000 feet tall.

Airplanes are not normally operated at temperatures colder than 30 degrees below zero because mechanical parts have more of a tendency to fail or break as they are more brittle, and engines are exposed to large internal temperature changes. Those temperatures can also be life-threatening for humans who may have to survive if they have to perform an emergency landing in a remote location. The federal government publishes a list of survival equipment that Alaska pilots are required to carry in their aircraft at all times. One of the original items was a rifle or shotgun. I still carry one on every flight for procuring game meat or surviving a bear attack. Alaskans carry survival gear in the bush, year-round, regardless of their mode of transportation. Modern electronics are popular because they allow contact with emergency services from anywhere on earth, with a small handheld satellite messaging device. Another essential in winter was a self-contained engine heater, in case you had to spend a night in the bush. But poor weather can delay rescue for days. Flying an airplane full of groceries ensured that I would eat well but only one way!

Sometimes, the airplane would be so packed with groceries that I could hardly see out of the windows. Even the copilot seat and floor were stacked high! The airplane was so heavy that it required me to keep it climbing after takeoff until I reached 11,000 feet so I could cross the mountains with a few hundred feet to spare. It took about a half hour to cross the most remote and rugged terrain, where I would likely not survive a forced landing. The Maule had a good heater, but the wisest pilot wears what he would want to be wearing as he runs from the burning wreckage! All that stuff in the back of the plane would be

CHAPTER ELEVEN: ALASKA BUSH PILOT

useless. Old pilots would say that survival gear is what's on you; the rest is camping gear. So I was pleasantly warm and comfortable, except for the first time I had to go to the bathroom really bad, but there was no place to land. Some guys can use their water bottles in flight, but I just can't get straightened out enough with all that heavy clothing. With no other option, I landed in a pass and watched my skis sink into the deep snow. After I relieved myself, I hopped back in and took off. It was a very long takeoff run, and I finally got airborne with little room to spare. From then on, I drank very little before the flight and absolutely no coffee!

Another time, I made it to the village but had to go really bad. So I didn't circle to announce my arrival as I usually did, but quickly landed and parked on the far end of the airstrip, shut down, and jumped out. As I was relieving myself, a guy rode up on his four wheeler and asked why I had parked there instead of the usual place!

Also, on one of my first flights across the mountains, I had a scare and was afraid I would soon crash in a very bad place. Not a flat spot in sight and many feet of snow and jagged peaks everywhere. I had just leveled off and was cruising at 11,000 feet, heading to the village with a full load. Every pilot knows what sounds his engine makes, so would notice any sound out of the ordinary. Especially in stressful conditions like flying over enemy territory on a pitch-black night or over other areas where you might be forced to land, like over the ocean or in the middle of a mountain range. Suddenly, I heard a loud pop, and I instinctively checked my engine gauges and looked around for the best place to crash. My heart was racing. Then a second loud pop, accompanied by the odor of potato chips! I was carrying several large bags of them, and the pressure change from sea level had inflated them like balloons. When I realized what had happened, I pushed the throttle back in, relaxed again, and ate a bag of potato chips. Since then, when loading potato chips into the plane, I take out my pocketknife and poke a small hole in each bag.

So here's the drill. When I arrive at the first stop, I circle the village before landing, so everyone knows I'm there. After landing and shutting

Helicopters, Jets, and Bush Planes

down, I open the cargo door, grab the ubiquitous blue plastic tarp, and spread it out beside my airplane. Next, I place all of the packages of groceries on the tarp, with the bread, fresh fruits and vegetables, eggs and meats in separate areas. I also carry several cases of soda pop. The last thing I take out is the cash box, containing a few thousand dollars for change. The villagers always have a government check to make purchases with. I place the box, along with my price list and pocket calculator, on top of the horizontal stabilizer on the back of the plane. Now the store is open. The villagers called me the fruit man.

Soon, people start arriving on snowmobiles or four-wheelers. After I see that someone has finished shopping, I take my calculator and price list over to their little pile of groceries and add them up. Then we go to the cash box to take their check and give them the change. Eventually, the thirty or forty people are gone, and it's time to pack up and go to the second village. Since it's about noon, I take out my sandwich and eat it while doing my preflight walk-around inspection of the airplane. Then I repeat the process at the next village, about a half hour away, before flying back across the mountains to Willow. Usually, the mission is pretty routine, but things don't always go according to plan!

One winter, we had a long cold spell, over 35 below zero every day. It looked like a warmer period was coming, and since we hadn't been able to fly for a few weeks, Tom made a grocery run. After waiting for a few days, it wasn't getting much warmer, but the bananas were getting too ripe. So one morning, with a temperature of 30 below, we decided that would be good since it normally warms up a little during the day. So off I went. I noticed that it was colder than normal at 11,000 feet, so I had the heater running full blast. Arriving at the first village, I circled overhead, and after landing, taxied to the parking area. I shut down and threw the engine cover on to keep it warm. As I was spreading out the tarp and getting the groceries out, I wondered why no one was coming. I pulled my calculator out of my pocket and turned it on. I could barely read it. And my ballpoint pen wouldn't write. It was still too cold. Finally, a young man rode up on a snowmobile. I could see that his eyelashes, eyebrows, and mustache were totally covered with thick frost and ice.

CHAPTER ELEVEN: Alaska Bush Pilot

I asked where everyone was, and he told me that they weren't coming because it was too cold. I asked how cold it was, and he said 54 below!

Bad things happen at temperatures that low, and I had to go somewhere else immediately. I couldn't stay in this tiny village. So I quickly put everything back in the plane and headed for a slightly larger village that had a warm schoolhouse. The engine ran fine, but it was too cold for any aircraft to fly safely. Engines produce moisture and pressure that is normally released through a hose from the crankcase to the outside air. In extreme cold temperatures, this moisture can freeze, plugging the hose, causing excess pressure to damage the engine. I made it to Lime Village, covered the engine, got my sleeping bag out, and slept on the floor of the school. The next afternoon, it was warm enough to fly again, so I sold some groceries and flew back home.

Another day, after poking a small hole in the potato chip bags with my pocketknife, I flew to the village airstrip, sold my groceries, loaded up the remainder, and prepared to proceed to the next village. As usual, before climbing in, I got out my sandwich and walked around the plane. I jumped in and blasted off, and arriving at the next stop I unloaded the groceries onto the blue tarp. Then I reached in to grab the cash box. It wasn't there. I quickly realized that I had left it on the tail of my airplane at the last village! People were already choosing the groceries they wanted. I said that I had an emergency and had to go. I told them to just take what they wanted and could pay me later.

An hour after I had left, I arrived at the first village again and pulled into where I had parked before. I jumped out before anyone came out and retrieved the cash box and all the loose bills that were blown into the grass by my propeller when I left. I was so fast that I took off before anyone came out and asked what I was doing! Needless to say, I didn't tell anyone about it for a couple of years. I still have a few little secrets.

At Christmas time every year, Tom liked to put on his Santa suit and fly upriver to a lodge, where all of the local kids would assemble. He would bring a large black trash bag full of inexpensive gifts. It was a great opportunity for everyone to get together during the long, dark, and cold winter. Everyone looked forward to it. One year, Tom asked if

Helicopters, Jets, and Bush Planes

I wanted to take the flight, and I agreed. I had a bushy white beard, so I didn't need the fake one. He said I would make a great Santa Clause in the red costume. I told him that, no, I would be Mrs. Clause, and my wife, Fe, would be Santa! And our eight-year-old daughter, Kelly, would be an elf. So we flew out to the lodge, landing on the frozen river in front of it. We knew everyone there, and Kelly enjoyed handing out gifts to all of her friends who lived upriver.

In our little town of Willow, there are three Vietnam helicopter pilots. We are good friends, of course, and I even share a birthday with one of them. The other one lives a couple of houses away from me, on the same lake. After living in the cabin for eight years, and Kelly needing her own bedroom, Fe and I decided to build a house that had access to electric power and school buses. One morning, after dropping Kelly off at school, I went to the airport to have coffee with Eddie as usual. He knew that I was looking for a lakefront lot to build on, and he told me that his neighbor, a real estate agent, had stopped by and said there were three lots just listed for sale on Long Lake, and they would go fast. I called the number and spoke with the owner in Anchorage. She said that two were already sold, and she had a list of potential buyers for the last one. I told her that I wanted the remaining lot and would drive to her house with a check for the deposit. She said she would hold it until we got there. Two hours later, after arriving at the owner's home in Anchorage, we gave her a check for the property. The lake was a very popular place, and there were very few unimproved lots left. When one came on the market, it usually sold before you heard about it.

So after the owner accepted my deposit, my family and I went back to Willow to look at the property. The roads were still unpaved, and there were no "Lot for Sale" signs posted. So we pulled into a driveway near some wooded lots to get directions. We spoke to the homeowner through the door, and he told us where the lots were. He was planning a motorcycle trip to the annual rally in Sturgis SD with his buddy. They were the other Vietnam helicopter pilots! We still ride Harleys. Fe and I walked through the woods from the road to the lakefront and felt very lucky to have found a great spot to build our house on. Besides having the lake to fly on, with either floats or skis, across the road was a grass

CHAPTER ELEVEN: ALASKA BUSH PILOT

airstrip for wheels! For a few years, I had two airplanes and would park one on the lake and one on my lot next to the strip.

That summer in 2001, we had a house built on Long Lake according to my hand drawing on a piece of graph paper. With three bedrooms and two bathrooms, the 1,200 square feet was cozy but plenty of room for the three of us, especially when compared to the 600-square-foot cabin. One of the best features was a heated two-car attached garage. With the hour-long bus ride to school, I decided to drive the several miles, saving Kelly a wasted forty-five minutes of sitting on a bus each way. But no more heating the car engine with a weed burner! I didn't even have to take off my slippers. After clearing a building site, I had several large stacks of birch trees. With a wood-burning heating stove in the living room, we needed several cords of firewood in the winter. I kept tarps on the trees, and the wood lasted several years.

Before moving from the cabin, I sold my Jeep and bought a used 3/4-ton Dodge truck with a diesel engine. Then I had a snowplow mounted on it. Besides my driveway, I plowed a few others that helped pay for my fuel. Plowing snow is fun, so I enjoyed keeping everything cleaned up. Otherwise, with only even an inch of new snow on your driveway, walking from your vehicle to your house requires cleaning your footwear before entering.

The last winter in our cabin we had 50 below zero temperatures for ten days straight. Diesel engines will not start at really cold temperatures, so you need to keep the engine heater plugged in. With no electricity, and not wanting to rely on the weed burner every day, I called the heating fuel business in town and asked how they kept their diesel trucks warm. They told me that below 20 degrees, they idle them fast and leave them running all night. So I used my Army ammo can toolbox to push the gas pedal in a little and left the engine running for ten days. It really didn't use that much fuel!

I kept my airplane at the airport in the winter, so I didn't have to put skis on it, but I did. Even though the taxiways and runways were plowed, there was still enough packed snow to operate on skis. Skis open up practically unlimited access to otherwise inaccessible areas. Also, at the airport there was electricity! I bought a small 75-watt heating pad at the auto parts store and glued it to a flat spot on the bottom of the engine with silicone. Then I fastened the cord to the engine mount, allowing easy access to it. I kept it plugged in all winter, ready to go, and gave my friend, Eddie, a few dollars a month for electricity.

If you don't mind waiting, or don't have access to full-time electricity, you could just use a portable generator and a small ceramic heater, a hairdryer, or a popcorn popper! Just stick it in the engine compartment and put the engine blanket over it for an hour or so. In remote locations, a piece of stove pipe and a camping stove, or a portable propane heater, would be carried in the airplane for heating the engine. In the old days, the mail pilots would drain their oil into a bucket and place it behind the wood stove in the remote lodge where they were staying. The next morning, after breakfast, they would pick up their bucket on the way out to their plane and pour the warm oil into the below zero engine, which would make loud noises but cause no damage! Then it would start.

All of the numerous lakes in the area are connected by locally groomed snowmobile trails in the winter since they are all surrounded by houses, providing easy access to the backcountry. There is no requirement to use the trails. Riders from the lower forty-eight are surprised that Alaskans can just blast off in any direction. In their home state, they are required to stay on the groomed trails, some with one-way signs, speed limits, and troopers!

The Iditarod sled dog race trail runs right down the center of our lake, eventually reaching the major river trail system leading to Nome, a thousand miles away. Several dozen teams with hundreds of dogs go through over a couple of hours. Everyone who lives in the area, plus hundreds of people from Anchorage, go out to watch the teams and encourage their favorite mushers. Along with neighbors, I would take my burn barrel and firewood for warming up and folding chairs to place next to the trail. We had three snowmobiles by then, one with an attached sled to haul things with. Others would bring folding tables and grills for cooking hotdogs. The trail was less than 20 feet away, and occasionally, a team would come closer and stop in front of us, attracted by the odor of the food. The musher would eventually get them going

Chapter Eleven: Alaska Bush Pilot

again. They weren't allowed to receive any help, so we just watched and offered encouragement.

After all of the teams had gone through, Fe, Kelly, and I would ride our snowmobiles up the trail, passing the teams along the way, along with lots of other people running around on snowmobiles, and having parties on the river. Three hours and a 65-mile ride later, we would arrive at a lodge in the remote community of Skwentna. After checking into our previously reserved room and having dinner, we would wait for the teams to arrive at the checkpoint on the river, about a mile away. Most teams arrived around midnight, and onlookers were free to wander around and see the dogs and mushers as the race veterinarians checked them over. Then the mushers would load the previously dropped supplies into their sleds and proceed a short distance up the trail, away from the commotion, to bed down for a short night of rest.

With temperatures below zero and the long, black night, the big wood stove at the lodge felt great. I would get out of bed in the middle of the night and look out the window, checking for the aurora borealis. That time of year, the northern lights were common but not easily seen by town residents due to the city lights. Out on the river, with no lights and no buildings or trees blocking the sky, they were easily visible. There was a lot of activity at the first major checkpoint because of the lodge and the airport. Many people rode their snowmobiles there, but a lot of people flew their airplanes there, too. After a hearty breakfast the next morning, we hit the trail for the ride home, stopping to visit friends along the way.

Whenever we saw a dog booty on the trail, we would pick it up to add to our collection. Volunteers sew thousands of cloth booties for the hundreds of dogs that wear them to protect their feet from the rough patches of ice. Some of them invariably come off on the trail. They're all different colors. One winter, a visitor from another state came along and collected booties as souvenirs for her friends. She even put a few moose droppings in each one just for fun. Moose droppings are the grape-size winter moose poop that quickly dry out in the snow. Moose survive the winter eating only twigs and bark from the willow brush,

Helicopters, Jets, and Bush Planes

so the droppings are clean, dry, and odorless. Gift stores sell earrings made from them!

The last great race depends on hundreds of volunteers. A lot of them come from other states to work in the coordination center in Anchorage. Others prefer to work along the trail, including veterinarians and their assistants, dog handlers, short-wave radio operators, and checkers. A big part of making the Iditarod race possible is the Iditarod Air Force. It is made up of volunteer pilots who fly their own planes to deliver the thousands of pounds of supplies to the various checkpoints along the thousand-mile trail. Things like dog food, musher food, bales of bedding straw, booties, headlamp batteries, and many other things that each musher prepackaged and labeled weeks before. The airplanes also carry dogs that are worn out, injured, or have just lost their enthusiasm for the race, back to the starting point. They also fly all of the checkpoint volunteers where they need to go. I never participated in that effort, but sometimes I flew a musher's family members or anyone who wanted to follow the racers, out to a checkpoint. On one occasion, I parked beside a small yellow plane, with a one-person tent set up beside it. A young girl was flying her little two-seat Champ airplane alone, following the race teams to Nome, and sleeping beside her plane. When I went out the next morning, it was 38 degrees below zero! I was glad I had a room at the lodge.

In the fall of 2001, a buddy and I decided to go moose hunting north of Fairbanks, a few hundred miles away. We found a great spot to camp and hunt, several miles down a dirt road, in a pretty remote area. It was beautiful country, and we were having a great time, staying in his truck camper. After several days of hunting on foot, we took a break and went to visit a nearby camp to see how they were doing. They had a pretty elaborate setup, with a dedicated meat trailer and a couple of large RVs. They even had a television antenna that allowed them to watch the news and weather reports. The men were out hunting, but they had brought their wives to tend camp. While we were chatting with them, someone caught our attention, and we watched the passenger jets flying into the World Trade Center. Incredible! It definitely put a damper on our hunting trip.

CHAPTER TWELVE
US Government Pilot

Our house on Willow Lake was just a couple of lots away from my friend, Garland Dobson, one of the other two Vietnam helicopter pilots in Willow. So after coming back from the airport in the afternoons in the winter darkness, and seeing that his hangar lights were on, I would frequently stop by to have a beer and visit. After he got back from Vietnam and separated from the Army, he went to Alaska and became a state trooper pilot. At the same time, he flew in the Alaska Army National Guard. Now, retired from his career as a state trooper, and the guard, he was a part-time airplane pilot for the Anchorage office of the US Fish and Wildlife Service (FWS). One of his old guard buddies worked there, in charge of pilot training, and I met him while visiting Garland one day. He wanted to know what I did, and he already knew my background. He said that I should come work for the FWS as a permanent intermittent pilot. Garland was the only one in the United States, and I would make two of us. Due to our experience, and flight instructor certificates, we could help train the other pilots, but we would work from home and only when we wanted to!

So, in 2005, I was hired, and it turned out to be one of my best jobs ever. I first went to Anchorage and checked out their facilities. The aviation department was located on Lake Hood, home to the busiest seaplane base in the world. Alaska has millions of square miles of public lands, consisting of 90 percent of the state's land. The FWS is under the US Department of the Interior, and along with the National Park Service and Bureau of Land Management, manages the federal land through sixteen national wildlife refuges, or NWRs. The Alaska Department of Fish and Game (ADFG) manages the state land. With no roads to access the wilderness, it is done with boats and aircraft. There were about forty airplanes and pilots based at the various refuges across the state. The facilities in Anchorage, including a large modern hangar with offices, plus a refurbished WWII hangar, were in pristine condition, and the personnel were top-notch. All of the several airplanes there were in perfect condition, with the best equipment available. What stood out was that management didn't particularly care about your dress or your hair length. Other than that, it was a lot like the military, with everyone being professional and happy. And no more saluting and calling anyone sir! I could even fly my own plane to work.

There were various makes and models of light aircraft, which were common in Alaska because they were most suitable for operations on the tundra and lakes. Depending on the time of year, they were fitted with large tundra tires, floats, or skis. I was rated to fly practically all of them, and I had gained a lot of experience in bush flying with the Maule. Normally, I would plan to fly for the government for a week each month when I was in Alaska. Besides traveling around the state, doing game surveys or training pilots at the various game refuges, I participated in several seasonal pilot training clinics each year. The purpose of these clinics was to provide a week of concentrated training and qualification in aircraft operations such as off-airport operations, float operations, ski flying, mountain flying, and instrument flying. Usually, about a dozen instructors and pilots would attend. All pilots are required to be trained, recommended, and authorized to perform each type of operation. We would normally stay in a government camp that had cabins, sometimes in a remote location, meaning no roads or services. After meeting in Anchorage, everyone would fly out to the location on the same day. One airplane, with a large cargo capacity, would carry all of our food and drinks. It was always great flying and a lot of fun.

CHAPTER TWELVE: US GOVERNMENT PILOT

Most of the aircraft were tailwheel airplanes that were better suited to operating on bush airstrips. The most popular plane in Alaska for off-airport operations was the Piper Super Cub. The FWS had several. They could get airborne off dirt, snow, or water, faster than anything else. Only fourteen seconds off the water! The main drawback of the Cub was the small cabin. There was room for two people and a little survival gear behind the tandem seats. A similar aircraft was the Aviat Husky, which had a little bigger engine and a faster cruise speed.

For operations that allowed for longer takeoff runs, the larger Cessna airplanes were used. The second most useful airplane in the fleet was the Cessna 185. It is a tailwheel plane with four seats and a larger cargo area. It also has a more powerful engine and a faster cruise speed. Like the Cub, it works great on floats, wheels, or skis, so we had several of those. We also had several nosewheel planes, like the Cessna 206, with even more space inside, which was a great choice for operating from longer improved runways. A nice thing about water operations is that you can usually point into the wind, and on a large lake or river, you consequently have a long and flat runway if the winds aren't too strong.

Another airplane that was unique was the Found Bush Hawk made in Canada. It had the same performance as the 185 and had a tail wheel but as much capacity as the 206. An added bonus was a large cargo door on each side of the plane. So it was the first choice for hauling 55-gallon barrels of fuel and other bulk cargo.

In order to manage the various species of wildlife in the large refuges, the FWS established remote camps. They were used by the biologists who had offices in the city, to observe and do on-the-ground surveys of the animals in their habitat. The data was collected to measure the success of their various programs. It was the mission of all of the airplanes and pilots to move people and supplies, as well as to conduct aerial game surveys. These were done over several days, primarily with the Super Cub or Husky, the pilot in front, and a biologist/observer in the back. Several of the pilots were also biologists, both males and females.

The FWS had a well-equipped camp about a hundred miles west of the town of McGrath, in central Alaska. There was a main building that was used for gathering, and cooking and dining. Around that building were several two-person cabins, all with heating oil stoves. Plus equipment sheds and outhouses. The camp was built by a river that allowed float plane and ski plane operations. A snowmobile was available for grooming a winter runway.

Normally, all of the flying was done with a Cessna 185 on skis. One year, when I was the assigned pilot for a winter moose survey, the refuge manager decided to try a different approach, hopefully resulting in less time required. I would fly the people and supplies out from McGrath with a 185. But the survey would be done with a chartered helicopter flying the biologists. However, it would not be practical to have the slower helicopter fly back to the camp every time it needed fuel. One of my duties was to deliver it to them, in barrels. For that purpose, I also flew a Bush Hawk to the camp.

One larger cabin in the camp was called the pilot's cabin. After I got everyone flown out to the camp, the helicopter arrived. The pilot joined me in the cabin, and while visiting, I asked him if he had flown airplanes before learning how to fly helicopters. He said no, he just wanted to fly helicopters, so he went to a flight school in Arizona and borrowed 50,000 dollars to get his ratings. An Alaska helicopter pilot can make a lot of money, but he has to live in the field. Meaning not much time in a town. I asked him where he lived, and he pointed to his duffel bag. He said right there. An advantage is no rent and no truck payment. Or grocery bills, entertainment costs, etc. And like commercial fishing or north slope jobs, you have a pile of money when you get home. If you're single!

So the plan was for me to take barrels of fuel out to a prearranged frozen lake and drop them off for the helicopter. I would pick up the empty barrels from the previous flight on the way back. For hauling the barrels, I took the Bush Hawk with the rear seats removed. So I had two airplanes. We had a radio in camp for communication with the helicopter pilot. Everything went as planned for the first few days. Then one morning, when I tried to start the Bush Hawk, it would not

Chapter Twelve: US Government Pilot

fire up. The next day, a mechanic was flown in, but he determined that it needed new parts, and it would take a few days. The "shower of sparks" ignition system had failed. So now I had to fly the barrels of fuel out to the lakes with the 185 the old way. Not nearly as easy as with the Bush Hawk. I took the right-side front seat out, and could stand a fuel barrel up in its place, then fill it with fuel. When I flew out and landed on a lake, I had to get the more than 300-pound barrel of fuel out by myself. The right ski was not far from the door, but the barrel just missed it when I pulled it out by the top and let it drop into the snow, carefully staying out of the way! The empties were, of course, easy to load. During the week, the helicopter needed a required inspection. So the company flew a mechanic out, and he completed it in a few hours. No town break for the pilot. The survey was completed, but the use of a helicopter was deemed too costly, and inefficient with two airplanes sitting there!

One of the most remote game refuges was in the Aleutian Islands. Cold Bay was over 900 miles from Anchorage. It is mostly populated with government employees and has one long runway, built during WWII. Due to its length and location, it was designated as one of the emergency landing sites for the Space Shuttle Program. The refuge had an airplane in a hangar, but it was difficult to get a pilot who would be willing to live there. So pilots from other refuges, or pilots who were not assigned to a refuge, like me and Garland, would fly there commercially for a week or two when they were needed. The islands had few people and lots of game, especially birds, bears, and fish. Before I went there, I was warned about the weather. Due to the location and geography of the Aleutian Islands, the weather was extremely unpredictable, making it difficult to plan a flight ahead of time. During World War II, many aircraft and crews were lost due to the weather.

The first time I was sent to Cold Bay, out of the ten days that I was there, I was able to fly one day. Even that flight had to end early because of the wind. Another day hanging out in the bunkhouse watching TV. Thankfully, I'd brought enough snacks. One time, I flew back to the airport in my Super Cub, and because the wind was so strong, even though

Helicopters, Jets, and Bush Planes

my airspeed was the normal 60 miles per hour, my ground speed was only ten miles per hour. So after touching down, I stopped after rolling less than 20 feet! Fortunately, the wind was blowing straight down the runway, as a crosswind would have been dangerous or impossible. I taxied straight ahead to the taxiway that would take me to the hangar, but when I turned just slightly, the wind picked my wing up, threatening to flip me over, so I immediately straightened out again. While I was sitting there, not moving, contemplating how I was going to get the airplane to the hangar, the tower operator called me on the radio. He asked if I would like him to contact the inter-island airline and ask for assistance. Obviously, he had seen this before and was probably watching for me to come back from my flight. Everyone knows when there's a new guy in town!

I watched two young men walk across the parking ramp to my airplane, and with my engine still running, each of them grabbed on to a wing strut and held the wing down while I slowly taxied across the ramp to my hangar. After putting the airplane away and closing the hangar, I went to thank them for helping me get out of a bad situation. From then on, I was more conservative when planning a flight. I just felt like I should try to get some of the flights done after hanging out in the bunkhouse for a week. It's hard to not feel any pressure to fly when that's the whole purpose of your being there.

I enjoyed the brown bear surveys, and there were hundreds of bears. The islands didn't have trees, just low grass and bush-covered hills. There was a large lagoon that was protected from the open sea, and it was only a few feet deep. It was full of seagrass that supported lots of sea life. There were usually several bears wading around, looking for food. I enjoyed watching the females wading far out from shore, with their cubs following closely, and showing them how to get something to eat. During the survey, with a biologist in the back, I would spend all day covering the creeks in the refuge, observing and counting bears. All of the islands sloped to the sea, and they all had streams that would be filled with salmon when they returned to spawn. The reason that coastal brown bears get so much bigger than their inland brethren, called grizzly bears, is due to their rich diet

Chapter Twelve: US Government Pilot

of salmon. There are so many fish sometimes that the bears just eat the fat-rich brains and leave the rest. The area is far too remote for a person to go there just to fish.

There would be dozens of bears, which are normally solitary, lining the creeks, feasting on the fish. I was surprised to see a few wolves doing the same thing, with bears all around, but they paid no attention to each other. We saw dozens of bears every day during the survey.

One non-flying day, everyone at the refuge office seemed excited, so I asked what was going on. They said that the monthly passenger ship was coming in and would be there for several hours. During summer, a small ship would travel between the island communities, delivering cargo and passengers. The passengers were mostly birders, who were there to see the thousands of birds that nest on the islands, hoping to spot a particular species that they hadn't seen in the wild. While the ship was in port, the locals were invited to visit the onboard dining facility, considered a treat. It was like a floating restaurant! So everyone in the tiny community, with no restaurants, would go there for lunch.

Another day, one of the ladies at the refuge asked if I could accompany her while she picked the huge salmon berries that were ripe. The bushes were above her head, and she was worried about meeting up with a bear while berry picking. They loved the berries, too. So I escorted her with a twelve-gauge shotgun.

The islands have a large population of tundra swans. They are pure white birds that nest in the northern tundra. Most of their time is spent on the waters of the numerous lakes, even when sleeping, safe from predators. Every fall, they molt, shedding their old feathers to make way for new ones. During this short period, they are unable to fly. The FWS uses this opportunity to capture and tag and examine some of them to track their health and migration patterns. They also weigh, measure, swab for bird flu, and take blood samples from them. Some of the captured birds are taken back to the refuge, where a veterinarian and their assistants have set up a medical center in one of the buildings.

The method used to catch the swans utilizes two airplanes and several people. I would fly a Cessna 185 on floats, alone. A larger De

Havilland Beaver on floats would carry, besides the pilot, two biologists and an inflatable boat with a motor. After spotting a bunch of swans on a lake, I would land on the water between the swans and the nearest shore. If they made it to the shore, they would get away because, even though they can't fly, they can run across the tundra really fast. As soon as I landed, they would start paddling for the opposite shore. So I couldn't stop. I would keep the airplane on step at a high speed and race around the birds, corralling them in the center of the lake, like a cowboy herding cattle. It was a blast! While I had them under control, the Beaver would land on the other end of the lake and tie up on the shore. The biologists would then take the inflatable boat out, inflate it, and put the motor on.

Then they would hop in and race out to the swans that I had corralled. Charging into the middle of them and using a large fishing dip net, they would catch a few and take them back to shore. There, the swans were placed in individual pet carriers, and with their heads covered, they were very calm and quiet. After doing all the measuring and recording, most of the birds were banded and released. A few were put into my airplane, and I would take them back to the clinic, set up at the refuge. There, they were sedated and put on oxygen in preparation for surgery. The veterinarian would implant a golf-ball-size radio transmitter into them and sew them up. The six-inch-long wire antenna, pointing straight up, stuck out from the swan's back!

They were then allowed to recover for a couple of hours before I took them back to the same lake. After landing and parking on the shore, I took the swans out, one at a time, and carried them to the water. As soon as I set them on the water, they took off across the lake like nothing happened! Amazing. We did this operation for a week or so and then flew back to Anchorage. A couple of days later, I saw one of the biologists in their office looking at their computer screen. I asked them if they could see the newly released swans that had started flying again. She showed me one that she had been tracking, on a map. The swan had flown, nonstop from Cold Bay, Alaska, to Humboldt, California!

Another time, I was sent to Cold Bay to fly a VIP around. She was the assistant secretary of the US Department of the Interior. The

CHAPTER TWELVE: US GOVERNMENT PILOT

local native corporation wanted to trade some of their land for land in the refuge, and the government wanted to see the land and learn about impacts on the environment before making a decision. So I flew the official and her assistant to the area, pointing out the game migration routes and possible future road access to a village, etc. After seeing the land in question, she wanted to fly over the village of King Cove, across the bay from Cold Bay. It was only accessible by airplane or private boat. They also had a medium-sized hovercraft provided by the state. If the weather wouldn't allow the boats or small planes to operate, without a road to Cold Bay there was no way to transport a person with a medical emergency to Anchorage.

On the way there, I dropped down to 20 feet and flew over the beach. There were always interesting things to see that had washed in from the ocean. Lots of big orange balls that were previously attached to crab pots, a few boat wrecks, fishing nets, and occasionally, a dead walrus. If we saw one with a tracking collar on it, we would arrange to have it retrieved. The collars are expensive and are designed to be reused. Once the battery dies, it likely won't be found. Eventually, I climbed up to cross the hills leading to King Cove. From a distance, I saw spray from a blowhole, in the bay ahead. I told my passengers to get their cameras out as we were about to see something special. I circled a couple of hundred feet overhead while observing several humpback whales bubble-net feeding. The blue-green water was crystal clear and calm, so the view was incredible. We could see the whales clearly, even though they were fairly deep at times. They would encircle their prey, making a bubble net, before surfacing in the middle, mouths agape and water churning!

In Alaska, if you find a dead walrus on the beach, you can take the head with its long ivory tusks. After getting it recorded and tagged, a taxidermist can mount the tusks, and you can display them in your home. You are not allowed to ever sell them. One of the FWS pilots, who was based at Cold Bay for a while, took his personal Super Cub with him. On his days off, he would go exploring. One day, he asked one of the other employees if they wanted to go with him. They were flying low and slow over the beach, looking for anything they could salvage. They spotted a walrus tusk sticking out of the sand, so they landed next to it. It took them a while, but eventually, they got it out. After getting it on the plane and climbing aboard, the pilot started the takeoff. He applied the throttle, and after rolling a few feet, the passenger yelled for him to stop. He said that as he was looking at the airplane tire starting to roll, he saw a couple of inches of the tip of another tusk sticking out of the sand. So they got out and dug up a second one! It took an extra trip to retrieve it as the head and tusks were very large and heavy.

Some of the caribou herds in Alaska have over 100,000 animals in them. I have flown over areas with caribou covering an entire valley. Hunters who live in the villages can shoot as many as fifteen per season. The meat is excellent, and a caribou is easy to field dress compared to a moose because they are much smaller. The herds get so big because they are located in remote regions, far from major population centers. Not to mention how far they are from the nearest road! Normally, when a hunter arrives at a hunting area by aircraft, he is not allowed to pursue game until the next day, giving the game a chance to escape. But one of the herds was getting too large for the habitat. Usually, nature provides more wolves to keep things in balance. To avoid having animals starving due to a shortage of food, the FWS authorized same-day hunting. That would allow a hunter with an airplane to fly around until he spotted game and then land and shoot!

One year, the herd was only a few hours flying from home, so a friend and I decided to fly our airplanes there and get some caribou meat. Our planes had winter skis on them, but the snow where we were going was not too deep. We probably could have landed on tundra tires, especially since the landings would be on flat lakes. After arriving at the hunting area near Iliamna Lake, we began cruising the area. We soon spotted a herd that was crossing a lake in small bands. Caribou are constantly on the move, covering several miles a day as they graze. I started my approach, planning to land alongside the line of animals in the middle of the lake. As soon as I slid to a stop and shut the engine off, I jumped out and ran toward the line. When I was a sufficient distance away from my airplane, I got down on one knee, took aim, and

CHAPTER TWELVE: US GOVERNMENT PILOT

fired at one. The caribou have a knack for moving away from a hunter, to keep just out of range for a good shot.

So I missed. I mistakenly thought that I could just follow them and eventually catch up with some that were not moving very fast. After tromping through the deep snow for a few hundred yards, and sweating profusely, I could see that the plan was not working. So I walked back to my airplane to try again. As I stepped out onto the lake, I spotted something strange. It was about the size of a medium dog and very dark. It was not moving, so I walked to it and found a recently deceased otter! It had no obvious wounds, so I don't know what happened to it, but I decided to salvage the beautiful fur. I tied it onto the wing strut of my airplane and decided to deal with it later. Right then, I was after something much larger. The new plan was to hide behind a small hill and wait for the next band of caribou to come along.

We didn't have a very long wait, and after the animals got within range, my buddy and I shot at the same time. After field dressing them, we walked back to where our planes were parked, fired them up, and taxied to our caribou. That surely beats packing! We loaded them into our airplanes, along with the otter that was hanging from my wing, and blasted off for home.

One of the FWS summer mountain flying clinics was held near the town of McCarthy, located in the Wrangell-St. Elias National Park and Preserve. The location is famous for the Kennicott Copper Mine, a National Historic Landmark. McCarthy is a fairly remote town, and the 60-mile dirt road leading to it is filled with potholes, not good for RVs. You can't drive in town, so you park at the end of the road and walk across a footbridge to the town. From there, you can ride on a shuttle van to the mine for a self-guided or guided tour.

Our base was a camp several miles from McCarthy, which had a good grass runway and a main log building surrounded by several small sleeping platforms with canvas tents on them. As usual, all of the participants flew their airplanes in, along with one carrying the food and drinks for the week. Each morning started with breakfast, followed by a short presentation covering the flying hazards and how to deal with them to ensure safe operations. Then pilots and instructors were matched up, and afterward, everyone went their separate ways until later that afternoon. Most of the time allotted to the training was spent in the air, flying to increasingly difficult mountaintop strips to practice the proven procedures and techniques that would result in an almost routine and safe operation. Many of the glacier strips were one-way only due to the steep terrain on one end. So you would take off over the same route that you came in on.

The beauty of the national park is exceptional, with snow-covered peaks and glaciers in abundance. At midday, the crews would shut down their airplanes and enjoy the sack lunch they'd brought in one of the most amazing locations on earth! At the end of the day, the planes would stop at the runway in McCarthy to fill their fuel tanks for the next day. It was a short flight from there to camp.

Alaska's animals are monitored electronically, as well as visually. A lot of the game's movement is tracked by satellite. They are also counted by aircraft flying over an area and noting their location and other details. Soon, this mission will likely be accomplished with drones. The tracking collars that are placed on the animal's neck have a battery that lasts for a couple of years. They are placed on the animal by biologists, after being captured using a helicopter with a net gun. Some collars and transmitters require the biologists to be in close range to retrieve data that has been recorded on them. The most expensive ones continuously transmit data.

The way that I could find a collared animal required homing in on a beeping signal from the collar. I would take a biologist with me to operate the radio that was used to communicate with the collar. My Super Cub or Husky would have a four-foot vertical antenna mounted on the wing strut of each wing, forward of the leading edge. I had a selector button on the control stick in the cockpit, which enabled me to select which antenna was active. Flying in a large circle near the area where the game was expected to be, I would soon pick up a faint beeping sound. I would point the aircraft at the area where the sound was loudest, and then, alternating between the antennas, could home in on the sound, turning slightly toward the side with the strongest signal. If

CHAPTER TWELVE: US GOVERNMENT PILOT

the beeps were equally loud, I continued straight ahead. I would know that we were getting closer because the signal would get louder. If the animal was concealed in the brush, the signal would begin to weaken after I flew over and then away from the target.

Once I knew precisely where the animal was, I could make a few low passes and usually get them to move within sight. The biologists wanted to see the condition of the animal, but it wasn't absolutely necessary. I needed a bigger plane for one mission to find a pack of wolves. The biologist sat in the back of my Bush Hawk with a receiver, a laptop computer, and a short handheld antenna. After picking up the signal from several miles away, and across a mountain ridge, I proceeded to track the radio collar. I finally pinpointed where the pack, or more correctly where the collar was, and pointed out the clump of bushes as I circled above it. He then pointed his handheld antenna toward the bushes and said that he had a signal. A few moments later, he said that he had a lock on and was uploading the information that was stored on the collar. After that, he said that he was reprogramming it. They could adjust how often they wanted to record any movement. When the collar showed them remaining in one location for several days, it was assumed they had killed a moose and were feeding. Then the biologist said that he was finished, and we flew back to the refuge without even seeing the pack.

Another time, I was working with a helicopter north of Fairbanks, in the winter. I used my Cub to locate the wolf packs and often, I would see them on a trail, up to a dozen, walking in a line behind the leader. One time, I counted twenty-four! After pointing them out to the helicopter pilot, he would try to get close enough for a biologist in the back to shoot one of them with a net gun. Then he would land and drop off a biologist, to take his samples and measurements after sedating the wolf, then move on to the next one. I remember that one male wolf weighed 150 pounds. Once, after observing the activity while circling above, I saw a wolf and an unsuspecting biologist on converging paths. They were both headed toward a high spot, where the helicopter could pick the biologist up, and couldn't see each other. I watched them arrive at the top, and suddenly, both of them stopped, and standing still,

Helicopters, Jets, and Bush Planes

stared at each other for several seconds, before the wolf turned around and ran back toward the brush.

One year, Garland and I planned a hunt near the village of Ruby, hundreds of miles northwest, on the Yukon River. Google Earth showed a good airstrip for our airplanes, near the tree line, which means easy walking, where we could hunt for moose. When we got there, we found that it was a mining strip, with a well-established camp about a mile or two away. Mining companies can get a permit to build an airstrip near where they plan on mining on public lands. Because they built it, they think that they own it. And anyone else, including the actual public landowners, is not welcome. I have had them meet me with a gun after making a precautionary landing in poor weather! So we set up our hunting camp and surveyed the area. It was not particularly easy to hunt from our camp. Although we were more than a mile away from the mining camp, the miners, taking turns, would go out of their way to harass us. Just before dawn, they would run their four-wheelers all the way over to our little tents and run around a few feet from us to let us know that we weren't welcome there. Unbelievable! These guys were working for minimum wages, and we had zero impact on their operations, utilizing a public airstrip, yet they felt compelled to harass us! Humans' actions are very perplexing sometimes. I assume they were muckers!

One evening, while sitting in camp, having a beer and relaxing, a large male black bear walked out onto the runway a couple of hundred yards from us. I grabbed my rifle, which was hanging on my wing, and fired. He was a mature male, and the meat provided many excellent meals. I also had the beautiful hide tanned and made into a rug. It hangs on a wall in my airplane hangar. Tired of being harassed by the miners, we headed home the next day, leaving our gut pile on their "private" runway.

CHAPTER THIRTEEN
Alaska Aerobatics

One of the recurring training events required all Department of Interior pilots to travel from Alaska to the lower forty-eight every two years for flight training in spin and upset recovery. There were no providers in Alaska. The usual airplane used was the American Champion Super Decathlon, model 8KCAB. Being a high-wing tandem seater, it was similar to our Piper Super Cub and Aviat Husky. The main difference was that it was fully aerobatic and capable of safely flying in practically any attitude. One of the primary causes of accidents resulting in fatalities in light aircraft occurs when the pilot, usually flying too slow, inadvertently enters a stall, followed by a misapplication of the controls, which then causes the aircraft to spin and fail to recover before impacting the ground, in a steep nose-low attitude at a high rate of descent.

The inadvertent stall can happen when the pilot is distracted while looking at something on the ground, like a moose! In Alaska, this is referred to as a "moose stall." If you're at a very low altitude, you may not have time to recover. But if you're properly trained, and have even a few hundred feet of altitude, recovery is quick and easy. The cause of the stall is exceeding the wing's critical angle of attack. If you react to the stall quickly, by neutralizing the controls and lowering the angle of attack, the recovery is practically instantaneous. The fastest way to reduce the AOA is to push the nose down a few degrees by applying forward stick, and adding full power to gain a little more airspeed.

If you're not fast enough in applying the proper controls, you may then enter a spin, with the aircraft rotating rapidly in an extreme nose-down attitude. It's very disorienting, and inexperienced pilots will likely panic. Now you need several hundred feet of altitude, and the recovery procedure is a little more complicated. Pilots use acronyms to memorize procedures, using the first letter in the list of steps that need to be completed in a particular order. The spin recovery process uses the word PARE. This stands for power, ailerons, rudder, and elevator. The steps should be completed quickly, in order. Power idle, ailerons neutral, rudder opposite, and elevator neutral. The recovery happens quickly, and the moment the rotation stops, all that remains to be done is to neutralize the rudder, pull out of the resulting dive, and add power. Unfortunately, for reasons unknown to me, the Federal Aviation Administration does not require all pilots to receive training in spin recoveries. In the early years of aviation, all pilots were required to be proficient in spins and recoveries. Consequently, even certificated instructor pilots are not competent in spins. Also, only certain airplanes are approved for practice spins.

Spin entries and recoveries are a great confidence builder, and it is my opinion that all pilots should seek training in them. It has always amazed me that pilots will readily spend thousands of dollars on upgrades to their airplanes, with bigger tires, longer propellers, higher horsepower engines, lighter weight components, and wing modifications but will not spend a few hundred dollars on training that could save their lives and the lives of the innocent people who fly with them.

Another major contributor to the fatal accident rate is the failure to recover from an unusual attitude. They are called upsets and are due to weather or turbulence, flight control systems issues, or again, the pilot's misuse of the controls. During initial training, for other than military fixed wing pilots, most pilots never fly upside down but may inadvertently end up that way sometime during their careers. The recovery training involves the instructor putting the aircraft in an extremely unusual attitude and having the student recover to level flight. Most

CHAPTER THIRTEEN: Alaska Aerobatics

primary training aircraft are not designed for or authorized to be used for this type of flying. But the American Champion Super Decathlon is ideal. Many aerobatic pilots who perform in air shows today, first learned to fly aerobatics in a Super Decathlon.

After the second time that I completed the training, at different flight schools, I realized that it was a very standardized curriculum, and they even used the same model of aircraft. It was all very basic for me, having been a US Navy fighter pilot, flying high-performance jets in every possible attitude. Of course, I learned to fly military aircraft in a two-seat training plane, and spin and upset training was almost as normal as regular flying. So I decided to buy a Super Decathlon and go into business myself. I called it Alaska Aerobatics.

I sold my Piper Pacer in Alaska and soon found a Super D that looked good and called the owner. He was a medical doctor who had been in the Air Force, so we immediately connected. He lived in Detroit, Michigan, and kept his airplane in an old World War II hangar, at the Grosse IIe Municipal Airport. It had been a very large WWII pilot training base, formerly known as Naval Air Station Grosse IIe. My daughter, Kelly, took a week off from her nursing classes at the University of Alaska, and we flew commercially to Detroit. After spending the rest of the day with the seller, and transferring ownership, we stayed overnight on the base at the Grosse IIe Pilot House, which had been built in 1933 for senior officer housing and an officer's club. It is still in use today and typically hosts weddings and other activities. Very cool place.

The next morning, we pushed N775AC out of the hangar and took off, heading south. I decided to take the opportunity to visit my dad's family in West Virginia since we were so close. We met at the local general aviation airport, which only had a grass runway. I talked my dad's youngest sister, Darlene, into sitting in the back seat with me in the front, for a photograph. Naturally, I fired up and took off! Flying around the airport, I fought the urge to do a loop or roll, and she really enjoyed the experience.

Helicopters, Jets, and Bush Planes

The flight to Alaska took several days. I had flown the highway route through Canada once, and driven it a few times before, and knew the route and all of the airports pretty well. It was a first time flying the highway for Kelly, but she had driven the route herself a few times. The fuel capacity allowed for three hours of flying, with about an hour's reserve. After landing for a midday fuel stop, and a quick lunch break, I continued to fly another three hours before stopping for the night, even though the sun was up for sixteen hours or more in June. As usual, the locals would always offer a ride to a nearby lodge or motel.

One of the four most common VFR routes from the US through Canada to Alaska follows the winding but fully paved Alaska Highway. So most pilots flew over the highway, the world's longest runway! In the lower forty-eight states, most roads have power lines that are very difficult to see and avoid. In the far north, with few towns, there are few power lines or poles, not to mention tall buildings and antennas. With no ground controllers to call while flying, and rarely another aircraft in sight, the flight is very relaxed. As long as you don't attempt to fly in marginal weather conditions! The only times that I've ever been really concerned about my safety, other than in combat of course, was in terrible weather in a small airplane. In a large turbine or jet airplane with sophisticated equipment like radar and anti-ice systems, there's little concern about ensuring a safe outcome. Once you're in it, it can be difficult to just turn around and go back. Kelly and I were on no schedule, so if there was any concern about the morning weather reports, we would enjoy another day on the ground.

The beauty of the Rocky Mountains is always amazing, and the airplane provided great visibility in all directions. Having previously taught Kelly how to fly, she occasionally took the controls and gave me a break. There are snow-capped mountains year-round in the northern Rockies, and the highway route stays in the lower valleys, with the riverbeds and railroads. As I did before, when flying the highway, I landed at Toad River, BC, and taxied across the highway to fuel up at the pumps at the gas station. Next to the restaurant is the motel. If you arrive in the evening, a sign on the door says, "Pick a room that still has a key in the lock and check in at the office in the morning!" The single

CHAPTER THIRTEEN: Alaska Aerobatics

ladies who work there are all from the Philippines. They said that it's much easier to obtain approval to immigrate to Canada than to the United States. The owner would take them to the nearest community, Fort Nelson, BC, a couple of hours away, every month or so, to shop. The ceiling in the restaurant was decorated with hundreds of baseball caps. So I donated another one, from Alaska Aerobatics.

The rest of the flight to Alaska was uneventful, and we landed on the grass runway beside our house in Willow and parked in our driveway. After a couple of days resting up, I flew the Super D to my hangar at the Willow Airport a few miles away. Then I spent a few weeks practicing the maneuvers that I would be teaching, developing my curriculum, pricing the various courses I would offer, and getting business cards printed. I also got my state business license, designed my website, and had a nice sign made and installed on the front of my hangar. It had a pair of wings and Alaska Aerobatics with my phone number. My airplane had a beautiful red and white starburst paint scheme, with stars outlined in black, and wide black and white stripes on the underside of the wings. It also had matching wheel pants.

I purchased two parachutes along with the plane, so I found a parachute club that had a rigger that could inspect them as they were nearly due for recertification anyway. Each student would be instructed on how to egress the plane and safely deploy the parachute in the event of an unrecoverable situation. Which I never heard of happening but is required by the FAA. About the only thing that comes to mind is a midair collision or flight control malfunction as practically every situation possible can safely be recovered from. Aerobatic category airplanes are built to withstand much more aggressive flying and are able to withstand many more g-forces than a standard category aircraft. And they are equipped with a G-meter that shows exactly how much stress is being put on the aircraft as you are maneuvering it.

Practically all general aviation aircraft are certified for operations in the normal category, limiting them to 30 degrees in pitch and 60 degrees in roll. This is a fraction of the maneuvering envelope that any airplane is capable of operating in. Consequently, most pilots have never flown inverted or done a loop, roll, or spin. So if his airplane gets upside down from turbulence, he doesn't know how to recover. In recent years, after many innocent airline passengers were killed, the FAA finally required all airline pilots to be trained in UPRT, upset prevention and recovery training. I trained a few of them.

Since aerobatics can make an inexperienced pilot nauseous, I would start my lessons with various coordination exercises that are gentle but difficult for most pilots. However, any competent pilot can learn to do them with precision, with practice, making them a better and safer pilot. The three primary controls of an airplane are the ailerons, rudder, and elevator. I would see that many young pilots neglect the importance of the rudder, which is controlled by the pedals. Abruptly moving the elevator, or especially the ailerons, causes yaw, the amount varying with the degrees in angle of attack, which needs to be countered with the rudder. I would tell them that a person can play the piano without using their feet, but not very well. The same can be said about flying an airplane.

The more advanced and disorienting maneuvers would be done toward the end of the forty-five-minute lesson. After several lessons, the pilot could perform loops, rolls, and upset recoveries. And they could enter into a spin and then recover from it with confidence. Most inadvertent spins are fatal because of the pilot's lack of training. But again, the training is not required! And a spin can result from mishandling the aircraft in any attitude. I demonstrated this by beginning a loop. But at the three-quarters point over the top, 45 degrees inverted, I would pull the throttle back and add full rudder input with a full-up elevator, maintaining neutral ailerons, resulting in an immediate loss of control and an unusual attitude. But while holding these control inputs, the airplane would always stabilize in a normal upright spin in the direction of the applied rudder—pointed at the ground in a fairly rapid descent, while rotating toward the applied rudder at a fast but stable rate. I would have the student look at the airspeed indicator, which would stabilize and remain at or near the one G stall speed, which is only around 60 miles per hour in a light airplane. The simple PARE

CHAPTER THIRTEEN: ALASKA AEROBATICS

recovery would result in normal flight almost immediately. At the moment the aircraft stops spinning, the pilot only needs to neutralize the rudder pedals and gently pull out of the resulting dive before returning the power to a cruise or climb setting.

This applies to practically all light general aviation aircraft, but I demonstrated the same principles in a jet airplane. It was in a straight-wing jet, the North American T-2, and would not apply in a swept-wing aircraft. In the swept-wing F4 Phantom, if you enter an out-of-control situation, and applying recovery controls has no effect, you deploy the drag chute. If that doesn't work, you always have the final option of pulling the ejection handle.

The F4 Phantom had a select handle in the front cockpit that allowed the pilot to choose between eject and command eject. In the eject position, the RIO could pull the handle and eject himself. In the command position, either the pilot or the RIO could pull the handle and eject both of them. The pilot would choose the position of the selector. I usually chose the command select setting so that, besides trusting my RIO with my life, while trying to control the aircraft until the last second, I could just tell my RIO to "eject, eject." Because when you get a cold catapult shot, meaning the catapult system does not produce the desired output or an engine flames out on the CAT shot, you don't want to take your hands off the controls because you will be instantly out of control, likely putting you outside of the survivable ejection envelope.

It's funny how some facts can be burned in your brain, like the time between the rear seat ejection and the front seat ejection was 1.392 seconds in the Martin-Baker ejection seat. The rear seat would be ejected first, because the front seat rocket motor would injure the back-seater if it came out first. I never had to eject, but I did have my RIO hold on to the ejection handle and be ready for my command. There were two ejection handles in the F4. The preferred one was for high speed and required you to release the controls, put both hands up to the top of your helmet, grab the handle there, and pull the face curtain down over your face to protect you against the several hundred knots of wind as you came up out of your aircraft. The alternative was to pull the handle between your legs, which doesn't cover your face, but only requires a quarter-inch pull to initiate the ejection sequence. That's the one you pull when operating around the aircraft carrier or land base and flying at low speeds and low altitudes.

The ejection seats in the seventies required you to be within certain parameters to guarantee a full chute and a survivable landing. For example, if you had to eject during the takeoff run, if your nose gear collapsed, causing your trajectory to be tilted forward 10 degrees, your parachute would not get fully deployed before you hit the ground or the flight deck. The modern ejection seat would allow you to eject from a very low altitude, inverted, and survive. A gyroscope would direct the seat rocket motor to direct its thrust to immediately upright the seat and propel the occupant to a safe altitude before deploying the parachute.

If you ended up in the water with your jet, you had to blow the canopy open, unbuckle yourself from your seat, disconnect your G-suit hose, and make your way to the surface wearing your helmet, flight suit, boots, torso harness, and G-suit before you drowned. Good luck. A couple of years after I retired, the navy developed the HEEDS system, a very small container of oxygen that was attached to the front of your torso harness. It gave you twenty minutes of oxygen, time to maybe get to the surface.

CHAPTER FOURTEEN
Private Pilot

After fifty years of flying in the Army, the Navy, the airlines, a bush flying service, personal flying, and the US Fish & Wildlife Service, I decided, in 2016, to stop getting paid to fly. Meaning that I was not going to stop flying, but I would stop flying other people's aircraft and would not fly my own plane for money. I have always owned an airplane since I bought my J-3 Cub while in Navy flight school. Besides using my airplane to fly my friends and family to fun events, or myself hunting Alaska big game, I also taught a few people to fly and gave many rated pilots their required biennial flight reviews, or tailwheel training, aircraft checkouts or spins and aerobatics training. I still occasionally give a good friend a flight review and sign their logbook, but I don't accept payment. And visitors always get free flights to our cabin or a nearby glacier.

The Decathlon was a beautiful airplane and a blast to fly, but with only two seats and very little cargo space, it was not a very practical family airplane, so I sold it to a pilot in Fairbanks, Alaska. It was strictly a basic aerobatics trainer, or a personal plane for pilots who enjoy aerobatic flight, and with no flaps to allow for slower landing speeds, it was not suitable for bush flying. I still couldn't afford a Super Cub, so I looked for another PA-22 Piper Pacer. The performance didn't compare to the Super Cub, but there were four seats. If you removed the rear seats, you had a large cargo compartment. The Pacer had the same type and amount of steel and fabric, the same instruments and fuel tanks, and used the same Lycoming engine, but was about half the price of a Super Cub.

The author's Piper Pacer is parked at his remote cabin. The only other ways to get there are by boat in the summer or by snowmobile in the winter. It's about seventy-five miles from the nearest road.

The Pacer was very popular in Alaska, too. Most of them were originally built with tricycle landing gear and were called Tri-Pacers. Tailwheel airplanes make the best bush planes for several reasons, so most of what we call Pacers had been converted from nosewheel planes to tailwheel planes. Anyway, I have owned three of them. My current one, rebuilt to like new condition by my friend, Eddie Trimmer, has several of his FAA-approved modifications, greatly improving the utility of the airplane. Like the clear plexiglass seaplane doors on both sides that swing up with lift supports, instead of the original single metal door that opened forward and was on the passenger side, extended landing

CHAPTER FOURTEEN: Private Pilot

gear to get more clearance from the rocks and brush, extended flaps and wingtips for added lift, and several other improvements. Recently, I added 29-inch-tall Alaska Bushwheel tires on the main gear and a Baby Bushwheel tailwheel.

Many bush strips and other off-airport landing spots are just wide enough for the airplane to fit on, with tall brush or rough terrain on the ends. After landing, you normally continue to the end of the strip. To take back off, you need to turn your airplane around. If there's enough room to taxi in a circle with your nosewheel plane, there's no problem. But if you have to get it turned around by hand, especially by yourself on a slippery surface, that's a problem. With a tailwheel airplane, on dirt or gravel, you can just lock one wheel with the brake, and with a little power, you just spin around in place. Or if you stopped and shut down, before getting back into your plane, you can just lift the tail and walk it around.

There are dozens of approved modifications that pilots add to their planes as they can afford them, and if you want to add unapproved modifications to your plane, you can convert it to the Experimental Category, which is fairly common in Alaska. That comes with restrictions, of course, like you can't use it for commercial purposes, such as flying passengers or property for compensation or hire. But pilots who want to access the most backcountry do whatever they can to make their airplane land and then take off from the roughest terrain in the shortest distance. Then they have access to much more hunting country than others. Alaska is one-fifth the size of the lower forty-eight states, but 99 percent is wilderness, with only aircraft or boat access.

Alaska has hundreds of airports and airstrips but relatively few that have scheduled airline service. In the mountain valley where I live, there are about two hundred mostly private, unpaved airstrips where a small airplane can land, but as soon as you cross any mountains, there are just river gravel bars and a few other relatively flat areas without too much brush. With a float plane, you have thousands of lakes to land on, but the major rivers are just too fast and dangerous to use. Every major river has Alaskan Native villages along its length. There are only about 230 of them spread out over the state, but they all have a good gravel

Helicopters, Jets, and Bush Planes

runway, built by the state to ensure mail service or emergency services, and some have fuel available, although it's very expensive because it has to be flown or barged in.

As important as regular mail, is the subsidized bypass mail. This program allows bulk shipments, including groceries to be sent directly to air carriers, bypassing the regular USPS system. Villagers hundreds of miles away can call Costco in Anchorage and place an order. The store employees will gather the items and hold them for pickup, for shipping to the village. Even though the US Postal Service pays private airlines part of the shipping costs, it is still very expensive. Before the villages had airplane service, the mail and freight were delivered by dog teams. A team could consistently travel 50 miles per day. So there were lodges about every 50 miles along the major trails, and many of them still operate today, some as hunting lodges offering guided hunts, with transportation by bush planes, jet boats, or even horses.

In 2021, at seventy-four years old, I decided that I owed myself an expensive luxury. My own personal helicopter! The most popular helicopter trainer in the world is the Robinson R22, manufactured in California. Designed as a personal helicopter, it quickly became a primary trainer due to its reliability and low operating costs. It only has two seats, but it has excellent performance and will fit in your garage! I already had a hangar where I kept my Pacer, and the hangar door is ten feet high. The R22 is only nine feet tall, and the landing skids are six and a half feet wide. With a pair of wheels that fit on the skids, one person can easily push it in and out of a hangar. Most small helicopters have three main rotor blades, which take up a lot of width. The R22 only has two blades, which can be lined up fore and aft, making the helicopter able to fit into a very small space.

Another feature of the R22 is its simplicity, with no hydraulic system. Most helicopters are a mechanic's and owner's nightmare, with multiple major components, each with its own logbook and inspection or replacement times. The R22 only requires routine inspections and oil changes, until a time limit of twelve years or 2,200 engine hours is

CHAPTER FOURTEEN: Private Pilot

reached. To be used commercially, the helicopter must then be completely rebuilt to like-new condition. There are two options for the rebuilding. The helicopter can be disassembled, crated, and shipped to the Robinson factory in California, or a factory-approved Robinson overhaul facility can rebuild it.

Chuck Moore and Bob Nance, fishing for salmon on a remote Alaska creek. They previously flew a helicopter together as US Army flight school students in 1967.

A factory-new R22 price is about 50 percent higher than a newly rebuilt helicopter. I have bought many vehicles in my lifetime, but only a handful were new. I always chose to buy a like-new vehicle at a considerable discount and pay cash. So I started looking for an R22 that was recently rebuilt or one that was due for a rebuild. After an extensive search online, and not seeing anything in Alaska, I took a chance and called the owner of the only Robinson-approved overhaul facility in Alaska. I asked him if he knew of any practically new R22s for sale. He said no, but he had one that he could rebuild. It had been his own personal helicopter, a 1992 Beta, that he had purchased new, flown for exactly 2,200 hours, and parked it in the back of his company's large hangar, planning to rebuild it someday.

I asked if he would sell it to me and rebuild it for me, and he said yes. We agreed on a price, and I made a large deposit to be used to buy the overhaul kits, with all of the new parts and components, from the factory. Perfect! I got to choose the paint color, the interior color, and the seat covering and color. I ended up choosing viper red with gold numbers on the tail, black interior carpets, and tan leather seats. After six months of waiting, I finally got my beautiful red R22 with everything new or looking like new. I hadn't flown or even been within a mile of a helicopter since 1970, when I got out of the Army fifty-five years ago except for one week in the Navy reserve in 1982. The FAA requires ten hours in the R22 to be authorized to fly it solo. The flight instructor and I were both amazed that I could still hover, take off, and land! I was so tense and concentrating so much that I could hardly stand up after flying it for less than an hour. But eventually, I became more relaxed and competent, and with ten hours of experience in an R22, I flew it home and pushed it into my hangar.

Author's wife, Fe Moore, standing beside his helicopter after landing on an Alaska glacier.

CHAPTER FOURTEEN: Private Pilot

After three years and two hundred hours of flying it, I still love every minute. I feel a little bit like that teenager in the Army in 1967, flying a similar helicopter that could land just about anywhere. Like they say, at a certain point, you feel like you strap the machine on and it becomes a part of you. My wife, Fe, and I frequently fly it to our remote cabin or land beside a wilderness creek to fish. I also enjoy taking others for their first helicopter ride, like my daughter, Kelly.

Several years ago, in the fall of 2010, after experiencing many Alaskan winter adventures with airplanes and snowmobiles, Fe and I started driving our RV to Arizona for the winters, eventually buying a house in Yuma. I don't have any flying machines there, but I have a Jeep and a couple of Harleys that we enjoy running around with. I also have two great nephews and their families whom we love visiting and getting together with for the holidays.

Last year, I learned that my commanding officer in Vietnam in 1968, Bert Rice, was nearby. I spend summers in Alaska while Bert is in Montana, and we are friends on Facebook. He contacted me one winter day and said that if I was ever in Yuma, AZ, he would like to get together. I asked where he was exactly, and after he told me, I said that I lived within walking distance and could be there in ten minutes! What a surprise. It was great seeing him and remembering our time in Vietnam. I look forward to our meeting every year.

About the same year that I quit my part-time flying jobs, I got a Facebook post from Greg Bucy, my replacement as Diamondhead 50 Fire team leader when I left Vietnam in 1969. He and Bob Segers, another Cobra pilot, had been contacted by the Wolfhounds 2/27, Charlie Company, 2nd platoon and recently attended their reunion. According to Greg, the Wolfhounds had been trying to find me since February 1969, when their platoon had been nearly wiped out in a fierce overnight battle with a large enemy force. My Cobra fire team had been dispatched to their location after their position had been overrun, and several of their comrades had been killed or wounded. I wrote about it in a previous chapter. I remember the mission well but never imagined that I would ever get to meet any of those soldiers in person. But forty-five years later, thanks to the internet, it happened! Seeing the same men who were on the ground that dark night, fighting for their lives, with many of their friends lying around them dead or wounded, was an incredible experience.

They had already had several reunions before they located me, Greg, and Bob, but they accepted us as their brothers at our very first meeting. Every one of them speaks highly of the Cobra pilots and personally thank us every time we meet. Their getting together after almost forty years was primarily due to the efforts of John Quintrell, who everyone called Big John. He was in the second platoon and, with help from his son, Tim, put in a tremendous effort in making the reunions an amazing experience for all of the Wolfhounds and their families who attended them.

That first reunion was a very humbling experience for me. Right away, I noticed that several of the Wolfhounds had been severely injured in Vietnam, with missing or damaged limbs and injured eyes. In fact, only two of the original members of the second platoon managed to complete their requisite full year in Vietnam. One of the wounded was Tommy Clack, an amazing man. He was an artillery officer with the Wolfhounds in 1969. A rocket-propelled grenade exploded at his feet, removing most of both legs above the knee and one arm and shoulder. Incredibly, he survived, and after many surgeries and years in hospitals, he is now a very sought-after public speaker throughout the country. He lives in Georgia and drives his specially equipped van throughout the eastern states. Another Wolfhound who has become a very close friend is Arie Hill. My wife, Fe, and I spent an entire winter with Arie and his wife, Nancy, whom he married soon after returning home from Vietnam, at their home in Florida.

Even though for years I felt like my contribution to the war was not particularly significant, I have never been treated so special. Big John has thanked me several times for saving his life and the lives of others that night in February 1969. Knowing what destruction a Cobra fire team can do to an enemy force, others told me that when they saw us coming, they started yelling and giving high fives to each other,

CHAPTER FOURTEEN: PRIVATE PILOT

realizing that they would get a break from hours of fighting. While my wingman and I were shooting rockets, grenades, and miniguns at the enemy, the second platoon could get behind some sandbags and eat some C-rations or have a smoke, reload their weapons, and relax just a little bit. I keep in touch with several of the guys and proudly wear my Wolfhound T-shirts almost every day. Fe and I look forward to every reunion and hope that we are able to attend many more. But we are all getting old and half of all Vietnam veterans have died, as of September 2024.

I've lived in sixteen states, one foreign country (Vietnam), and visited many others. The world is an amazing place, but America is the best!

So far, my life has been a great adventure, and I wish it would never end.

www.ingramcontent.com/pod-product-compliance
Lightning Source LLC
Chambersburg PA
CBHW061310110426
42742CB00012BA/2128